50 Hikes in Northern New Mexico

50 *Hikes*

In Northern
New Mexico

From Chaco Canyon to the High Peaks
of the Sangre de Cristos

First Edition

KAI HUSCHKE

The Countryman Press
Woodstock, Vermont

An Invitation to the Reader
Over time trails can be rerouted and signs and
landmarks altered. If you find that changes have
occurred on the routes described in this book,
please let us know so that corrections may be
made in future editions. The author and publisher
also welcome other comments and suggestions.
Address all correspondence to:

       Editor
       50 Hikes Series™
       The Countryman Press
       P.O. Box 748
       Woodstock, VT 05091

ISBN 978-0-88150-680-8

Text and cover design by Glenn Suokko
Maps, cover and interior photos by the author

Published by The Countryman Press, P.O. Box
748, Woodstock, Vermont 05091

Distributed by W. W. Norton & Company, Inc.,
500 Fifth Avenue, New York, NY 10110

Printed in the United States of America

10 9 8 7 6 5 4 3 2 1

A cholla bloom protected by prickly spines in the desert.

■ WEATHER

Summer thunderstorms can be intense in northern New Mexico, whether you are hiking along grassy Latir Mesa or exploring the unique sandstone features of the Dena-zin Wilderness. These storms typically arrive in the afternoon, building incredible cloud banks that can unleash rapid-fire lightning strikes. Cells often will hover and send forth dozens of downstrikes in a concentrated area, particularly in areas like the Valle Caldera. New Mexico is one of the nation's leaders in lightning-caused injuries and deaths each year.

Do not take an approaching storm lightly, whether you are bound for the summit of Kitchen Mesa or hiking along the shoulder ridge of Truchas Peak. The best course of action is simple: Get yourself out of harm's way. In the mountains this usually means moving quickly to a lower elevation into the cover of the trees. You can also lessen your chances for trouble by checking the weather reports prior to your hike. And it's a good practice to be mindful of the time of day you start your hike and to scan for possible safety zones en route. On the high plateaus you should look for overhangs along cliffs and rock outcroppings or, better yet, return to your vehicle before bad weather arrives.

Temperatures can drop 20 to 30 degrees when a thunderstorm cell passes overhead. In the high plateau country this could mean going from 90 degrees to 65 degrees in an extremely short amount of time. Though this is a big swing, it isn't too severe a threat to your wellbeing. However, in the mountains a 20-degree drop could mean summer temperatures sinking into the 50s or 40s, where the threat of hypothermia is greater if you aren't properly prepared for rain. Temperatures often plummet to the freezing level and beyond in certain high elevations in the summer, turning rain into snow.

Of course, elevation always brings somewhat cooler temperatures. A simple equation to remember is that the higher you climb, the cooler the temperature. Always carry proper rain gear and clothing layers to stay dry and warm. The National Oceanic and Atmospheric Administration web site (www.noaa.gov) provides accurate weather forecasts for any area you plan to visit. Local ranger stations and/or information centers also are key resources for obtaining weather forecasts. (See Resources for phone numbers and web addresses.)

Flash flooding in the high plateau is truly an amazing spectacle. In a matter of minutes trails can become raging creeks, and arroyos that were bone dry prior to a storm suddenly become swift-moving rivers. Avoid getting caught in any canyon settings when these sorts of storms are threatening. Also, fording creeks and arroyos that are running mad would not be wise. Even a smaller arroyo may be unsafe because you might be swept downstream into a larger one that could be running much faster and deeper. It's better to wait it out, preferably somewhere sheltered, than to chance it.

Make sure to have proper protection from the sun too, especially with the high-elevation UV intensity of northern New Mexico. And proper hydration is an absolute must, because summer temperatures are often more than 100 degrees in the high desert.

■ GEOGRAPHY

The two most prevalent hiking zones in northern New Mexico are the high plateau desert and the subalpine. Each has specific obstacles and considerations. In the high plateau you are faced with two primary concerns: exposure and dangerous plant life. Exposure plays itself out in the intensity of the sun and the power of thunderstorms. There are a number of plants with defensive measures—Russian olive thorns, prickly pear cactus spines, and the yucca's sharp points—that will keep you on constant guard, especially if you are moving off-trail. In the subalpine, negotiating downfall and scrambling up loose rockslides represent possible hazards. In both zones the altitude is surely a hazard, especially if you are not acclimated. Altitude sickness can strike you at an elevation of 8,000 feet and surely more so the higher you climb into the mountainous zones of northern New Mexico. Pulmonary and cerebral edema can also occur at elevations as low as 9,000 to 10,000 feet. The most important action to take if either occurs is to retreat to a lower elevation immediately. It is also critical to stay hydrated when at altitude.

Perhaps the most threatening hazard isn't being stuck by cholla or tripped up by a tree root, but rather being directionally challenged. The hikes here are mostly enjoyed via trail systems that mitigate this geographic risk. Some areas lack designated trails, and you must always be aware that trusting a trail alone isn't the best way to enter more remote backcountry settings, or even a relatively short day hike for that matter. A map and compass or GPS are invaluable allies in keeping you grounded in relation to your environment. Always carry one or the other, and check the map periodically to confirm your location.

ANIMALS

Our separation from wild animals in everyday life has come to mean that many of us fear desert, forest, and mountain inhabitants like the rattlesnake, bear, and cougar. But the reality is that the chance of a violent confrontation with an animal is extremely remote. Watching a black bear feeding in a high mountain meadow is a fantastic experience. If you feel the distance between you and the bear isn't far enough, make some noise to warn it of your presence. A bear will acknowledge you by moving away or keeping a watchful eye on you while it continues to feed. If you want to know more about how you can minimize an encounter with large wild animals, read *Don't Get Eaten: The Dangers of Animals That Charge or Attack,* by David Smith.

Rattlesnakes inhabit a number of places referenced in this book, so it's important to watch where you place your hands and feet. If you do encounter one, keep your distance and don't provoke it. Pay special attention when you are near overhangs and boulders or along arroyos. The same precaution goes for scorpions. If you are camping make sure to check your sleeping bag, tent, and shoes for either of these creatures.

The surest way to attract unwanted animals is food. Marmots, squirrels, mice, birds, pack rats, and other smaller, seemingly less threatening creatures actually may give you the most trouble. So keep your food stored properly. If you are camping in the mountains, be sure to secure all food off the ground if possible. Cook away from tents and try not to leave any food unattended inside your tent.

KEYS TO BEING PREPARED

The two most emphasized and hopefully adhered-to credos for hiking and backpacking are the Ten Essentials and Leave No Trace. You should also pay attention to planning, rules and regulations, equipment, and trail etiquette.

TEN ESSENTIALS

Maps and trail information
Compass
Flashlight/headlamp
Extra food
Extra clothing
Sunglasses
First-aid kit
Knife/multitool
Matches/lighter
Fire starter

LEAVE NO TRACE

Leave No Trace is the philosophy of minimal impact and removal of any obvious signs of human presence. Stay on trails, use existing campsites, camp 200 feet from water sources, pack out solid human waste or utilize cat holes, don't remove branches or cut down trees for firewood, don't disturb the plant and wildlife, and pack out what you pack in. The idea is a simple one—leave the wilderness as you found it or better. More information can be found at www.lnt.org.

PLANNING

It is always a good idea to find out the conditions of the area you plan to visit: weather, road access, and trail conditions. The Resources section at the end of this book lists the agencies that manage public land in northern New Mexico, and the people who work there should be able to answer all of your questions. Another im-

Northern New Mexico holds a surprising number of beautiful high mountain lakes.

portant element of backcountry travel is to leave your plans with someone back home in case of an emergency. Provide them with dates, places, and contact numbers, along with a time frame for notifying the proper agencies if you don't return. Remember, it's better to be safe than sorry.

RULES AND REGULATIONS

The hikes discussed here run through national monuments, wilderness areas, state parks, wildlife refuges, private reserves, natural areas, and national forests. Each of these areas has its own rules and regulations. For instance, wilderness areas have maximum group sizes of 12, allow a maximum of 14 days at any one campsite, and have a rule against mechanized travel (cars, motorcy-

cles, bikes, hang gliders, etc.). National monuments have restrictions on horse use, access for dogs, preservation of natural or archeological features, and typically require an entrance fee. To access the Valle Caldera, you must sign up in advance and prepay a fee of $10. Always verify the current rules and regulations with local management offices before hitting the trail. The information provided throughout this book is a basic overview, and should answer the questions of the average hiker or backpacker.

EQUIPMENT

What should I wear? What should I bring? The answers to both of these questions obviously hinge on where you are going and for how long and your own personal tastes. No matter where you go, remember that function and comfort, not fashion, are the keys. The following is by no means a comprehensive list, but it does offer a few suggestions and reminders.

If it feels good, wear it. But try to select clothing items made with synthetic material instead of natural fibers. These materials are more comfortable, dry quickly, usually have better breathability, and retain heat better than wool or cotton. Straight wool isn't bad, but definitely avoid cotton. Cotton doesn't dry quickly, can cause hot spots and rashes when it becomes wet with perspiration, and robs you of body heat when wet in a cold environment.

Good hiking socks are well worth the money. Most are made completely of synthetic material or a blend of synthetics and wool. Good socks pad your feet in the proper places, dry quickly, and hold their shape, a good characteristic when you're on a long trip.

When walking in rugged terrain, going cross country in the high deserts, in wet or snow conditions, or when carrying a backpack on a longer outing, hiking boots provide sound stability and reduce leg fatigue. However, low-cut hiking shoes, trail-running shoes, and even good running shoes are adequate for many of the hikes listed here. These types of footwear are far more comfortable than heavy hiking boots, and when you're carrying a light load or day-hiking, they'll make your legs feel much livelier during and after the trip.

PACKS

I recommend looking for a backpack the same way you should look for a new bicycle: focus on fit over everything else. The price range between specific packs is vast, differentiated by the quality of materi-

als, design, and features offered. A moderately priced backpack should have enough adjustment points to gain a good fit, be constructed of reasonably good material that will last many hiking seasons, and be outfitted with features that make sense considering the demands of backpacking. I don't mean to steer you toward one kind of equipment store over another, but specialty outdoor stores are more apt to have personnel who actually hike and backpack and can help you find a pack for your specific body type.

Day packs, fanny packs, and larger hydration packs are great for day hikes. Most are big enough to carry a supply of water, food, clothing, and other provisions. Fit is still important, but it isn't as crucial because of the minimal amount of weight being carried.

HIKING POLES

There was a time, not too long ago, when the elderly were the only people you saw hiking or backpacking with walking sticks. But these days all age groups are enjoying the benefits of adjustable hiking poles with ergonomic grips that transform into a monopod for your camera. Whether or not the poles are cluttered with features or made of the latest lightweight alloy, their use makes sense for hikers and backpackers of all abilities.

Day-hiking or backpacking is much more enjoyable and energizing with poles (old ski poles do the job and cost a lot less). The poles keep a portion of your pack's weight off your legs, keep your arms swinging to aid circulation, and help pull you uphill and absorb some of the impact going downhill. And if you stumble, your extra set of "artificial legs" can help you avoid a face plant.

WATER PURIFICATION

It is a good idea to bring at least two methods of water purification with you on long day hikes and backpack trips. I recommend a good pump-style system (there are a variety to choose from) and emergency potable water tablets.

DUCT TAPE

This item should be the eleventh essential. Duct tape is perfect for everything from repairing a pack or a hole in a sock to a cracked flashlight case. It also can serve as a substitute for gaitors or to cover hot spots or blisters on your heel. You could carry a whole roll (somewhat heavy) or just wrap a decent amount around the shaft of your hiking pole or water bottle.

HEADLAMPS

Almost all the headlamps on the market today utilize an LED light that burns brighter and longer than conventional bulbs. But they still require AA or AAA batteries. When you aren't using your headlamp, or are storing it between hiking seasons, it's a good idea to reverse the battery positions (positive and negative). This way, if you accidentally turn on your headlamp while reaching into the top of your pack for candy, you won't drain the batteries.

MOUNTAIN FOOD

Buying dehydrated foods can be quite expensive. If you backpack a lot, then a food dehydrator and vacuum-sealing machine are well worth the investment. Fruits like apples, pears, plums, strawberries, peaches, and bananas make great trail snacks, and dehydrating them on your own saves money. Vacuum-sealing and freezing the food items will help keep them fresh two to four times longer.

Whole meals also can be dehydrated or just vacuum-sealed and frozen without dehydration. When you're ready to hike, just remove the non-dehydrated, premade meal from the freezer, and keep it frozen in a cooler as long as possible before you step onto the trail. These meals should be fine for a number of days after they have thawed as long as they're stored in a vacuum-sealed bag. To heat your dinner, just drop the package into boiling water. For more information on dehydrating different kinds of foods, check out the *Complete Dehydrator Cookbook,* by Mary Bell and Evie Righter, published by Morrow Cookbooks.

TRAIL ETIQUETTE

Your reasons for wanting to hike in the outdoors probably aren't much different from those of other people who may have chosen the same place you did. If you keep this in mind, it will be much easier to observe proper manners afield. When you encounter people on horseback or leading a pack line, you need to yield the right-of-way. Whether the riders see you first or you see them, make sure to say "hello" or "hiker up," not so much for the riders but so the horses know that the object in the trail ahead is a human (yes, horses can be a little slow in the head). Give a horse plenty of room to pass; if the trail isn't wide enough, step off on the downslope side. If the horse gets spooked by you or something else while passing, it will turn away (upslope) from you, which should make it easier for the rider to gain control.

HIKE OFF-DAYS/SEASON

Weekdays, whether at the height of the season or on either end, are a great time to venture out while avoiding the additional weekend trail traffic. On the back half of the

1

Cabezon Peak

Type: Day hike

Season: March to November

Total distance: 2 miles

Rating: Easy

Elevation gain: 150 feet

Location: Cabezon Peak Wilderness Study Area, 27 miles northwest of Bernalillo

Maps: USGS Cabezon Peak

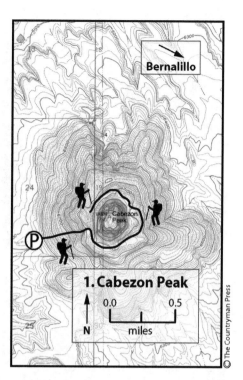

Getting There

From Bernalillo, take US 550 24 miles northwest to San Ysidro. Approximately 18 miles north of San Ysidro (42 miles total), turn left onto CR 39 at a sign for San Luis. At 8.7 miles along CR 39, the road surface changes from pavement to dirt. At 13.1 miles (55.1 miles total), the road splits. Take the left fork, which crosses over a bridge in less than 1 mile. After the bridge crossing, drive another 2.2 miles to a sign for Cabezon Peak and the access road to the parking area and trail, another 0.9 mile (59.2 miles total).

The Trail

As Cerro Pedernal (located near Ghost Ranch) scrapes the sky in distinctive fashion above the Chama River valley and be-

Cholla below Cabezon Peak

50 Hikes in Northern New Mexico

yond, so too does Cabezon Peak (7,786 feet), its gumdrop shape acting as the sacred beacon of the Rio Puerco valley. The Navajos tell the story of a giant who was slain on Mount Taylor (11,301 feet), with the lava flows and a collection of more than four dozen volcanic necks representing the aftermath. The area around Cabezon is part of the Mount Taylor volcanic field, which was created over millions of years as eruptions sent mud flows racing down the slopes of Taylor and lava out across the landscape from a number of outlets, including Cabezon Peak. The slopes run steeply off Cabezon as they transition from thick blankets of loose rock onto a pedestal base of juniper, yucca, and cholla before slipping steeply again to claw tracks of arroyos with open grassland radiating outward.

Cabezon Peak, literally "big head" in Spanish, is one of 50 volcanic necks in the area. These were formed by molten lava pushing through rock layers of an ancient sea. As is often the case with the amazing geology visible today, it took millions of years for the softer sedimentary rock to be broken down and carried away in order to expose the harder basalt that is Cabezon and the other headless necks in the area.

A trail, measuring approximately 1¾ miles, hugs the bottom end of the loose rock slopes as it circles the benched pedestal of Cabezon. The trail meets a fenceline on the northwest side of the mountain. Even from the benched area, you have high views across the Rio Puerco valley to the Sandia Mountains to the east, the southern end of the Jemez Mountains to the north, and to the west and south an encampment of the some 50 other volcanic memorials.

The entire wilderness study area encompasses 8,159 acres, which means there is plenty of cross-country exploring to do beyond the lower slopes of Cabezon. Following rainy periods in the warmer months of the year the sun-leathered ground will transform into a colorful scene, with cholla sprouting delicate fuchsia blooms, prickly pear showing yellow flowers, and a nice collection of desert wildflowers, from aster to sunflowers to penstemon, revealing other attractive shades.

Be the Hair on "Big Head"

Scramblers, you're in luck. Starting on the east side and moving slightly north at points via a number of steep scrambles, you can reach the top of Cabezon Peak. To do this you must be in good physical condition, have some knowledge of climbing in loose rock terrain, and have the smarts to wear a helmet. As you would expect, the sky and landscape shine with even greater brilliance from the summit.

2

Ojito Wilderness

Type: Day hike or overnight

Season: March to November

Total distance: Variable

Rating: Easy

Elevation gain: 200 feet

Location: Ojito Wilderness, 25 miles northwest of Bernalillo

Maps: USGS Ojito Spring and Sky Village NW

Getting There

From Santa Fe, travel south on I-25 for approximately 40.5 miles to Exit 242, signed for Bernalillo and US 550 for Cuba. Take US 550 toward Cuba. At 21.2 miles turn left onto Cabezon Road (look for mile marker 21; there is also a sign for the Ojito Wilderness). The road surface is dirt and packed gravel. Stay left at the fork less than 0.1 mile down the road. At 4.5 miles (25.7 miles total) you reach the parking area and trailhead for White Mesa. After crossing a wide arroyo at 5.7 miles the road forks again; stay to the right. There is a sign for the Ojito Wilderness at 9.3 miles (30.5 miles total). There are a couple options for parking: Beyond the wilderness sign there is a small turnout about 0.2 mile down, and a parking area at 0.5 mile.

The Trail

Seismasaurus once stepped across this area at an estimated height of more than 40 feet and weighing in excess of 70 tons. Fossilized remains were excavated from a location not too far from the parking area, and they are currently on display at the New Mexico Museum of Natural History and Science. Stone tools, pottery chards, and petroglyphs that date back to the Paleo-Indian period have been discovered in certain areas of the wilderness. Tamarisk chokes arroyos, delicate wildflowers spread themselves out in lacy whiteness between juniper and yucca, elk graze the grassy zones, and rattlesnakes hunt in the cool of the night. Cabezon Peak and a city of volcanic necks stand to the northwest, while sunflowers bloom across the often-parched earth. These are but a few of the many dimensions of the Ojito Wilderness.

The 10,903 acres of wilderness terrain

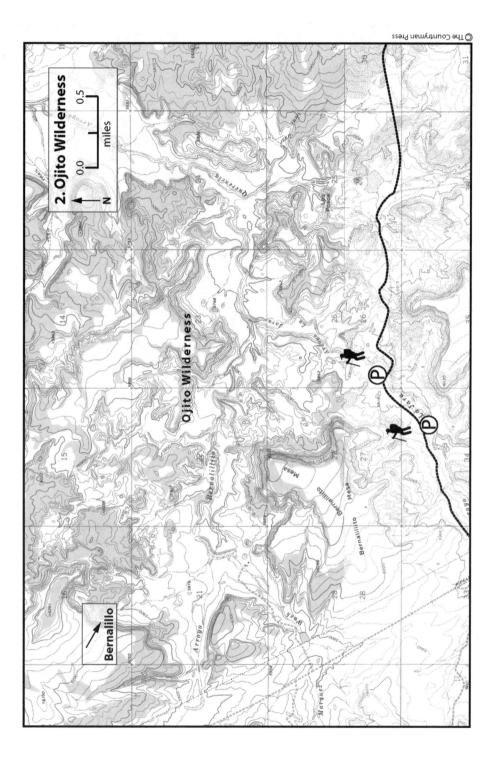

A rattlesnake in the Ojito Wilderness

are a mix of arroyos of various sizes, some with richer collections of plant species growing along the bottoms, along with rock outcroppings and mesas. The most prominent mesa is Bernalillito Mesa, which runs along the western edge of the wilderness area. The dominant vegetation consists of sage, chamisa, prickly pear cactus, juniper, yucca, cholla, and a range of wildflowers like aster, zinnia, and paintbrush. Rain always will bring things to life, sprouting meadows of desert wildflowers as well as the delicate fuchsia-colored cholla blooms.

The options for exploring this trailless zone, officially designated a wilderness in 2005, range from walking along sandy arroyo bottoms to cutting across open spaces landminded with cactus—please don't disturb the cryptobiotic soil—and decorated with hoodoos to clambering up the pinion pine mesas for a high view of the area. Multicolored rock bands are joined by colorful ground cover during the wildflower seasons.

There is very little relief from the intensity of the sun here in the desert, so hike early in the day and/or in the cooler months of the year. Animal life is vibrant, with mammals like the coyote, elk, pack rat, cottontail rabbit, and mountain lion calling the Ojito home. There are also many different kinds of insects and a handful of reptiles, the most notable being the western diamondback rattlesnake. Often you will find these snakes near water sources and in shaded places under rocks.

Water works the terrain in many ways: providing sustenance, reshaping arroyos by striping away the soft soil, and at points leaving behind rocks balancing on small towers of soil. When you reach some high ground, in the distance you can see the Sandia Mountains to the east, the southern end of the Jemez Mountains to the north, and the prominent rounded haystack-shaped feature to the west that is Cabezon Peak, a volcanic neck originally formed some 2 million years ago.

Tamarisk, also known as salt cedar, grows to heights of more than 15 feet tall in the arroyo bottoms and is distinguishable by the fuzzy, feathery, coral-like leaves and its 2-inch-long bottlebrush blooms, which show in summer. Along the edges of some of the arroyos you may find small barrel-like cactus clinging to boulders like mussels on shoreline rocks. The area is a mix of sedimentary rock, gypsum, volcanic ash, and volcanic rock. There are places where the white and red rock bands appear to have been carved out by a giant spoon. The Ojito Wilderness is an amazing place to wander and discover, whether you are searching for a fossil or pottery shard, or just the solitude of the desert.

Desert Duathlon

The White Mesa area is open to hikers and mountain bikers. A series of long, looping single-track and double-track pathways provide more than 15 miles of unique mountain biking here. The area has only recently been opened to mountain bikers, thanks in part to the efforts of a group called Friends of Otero, which is helping the Bureau of Land Management (BLM) maintain the trails and facilities. More information can be found at www.foomtb.org.

Tent Rocks

Type: Day hike

Season: Year-round

Total distance: 3.3 miles

Rating: Easy to moderate

Elevation gain: 600 feet

Location: Cochiti Pueblo (managed by the BLM), 25 miles west of Santa Fe

Maps: USGS Cañada

Getting There

Take I-25 south from Santa Fe toward Albuquerque for approximately 17.5 miles to Exit 264. Then head west on NM 16, signed for the Cochiti Pueblo. At 26 miles total, or 8.5 miles along NM 16, you reach a T-intersection. Turn right, now driving north along NM 22. In approximately 0.2 mile you will see a brown recreation sign marked KASHA-KATUWE/TENT ROCKS. At 2.7 miles along NM 22 (28.7 miles total) you turn left, continuing now in a more westerly direction along NM 22. There are signs again for Tent Rocks. At 30.4 miles, turn right onto FS 266. The road surface changes from pavement to gravel in 0.3 mile. You reach the picnic area and trailhead for Tent Rocks 4.6 miles along FS 266 (35 miles total). There is a daily fee of $5 per vehicle or you can display your National Parks Pass.

The Trail

No matter whether you harbor childhood thoughts of elaborate oceanside sand castles, visions of exotic treks in central Turkey, or fantasies of exploring distant planets, Tent Rocks will match anything you can imagine. What you see today took millions of years to form, and native peoples have appreciated the striking uniqueness of the area for more than 4,000 years. For you, it will take a full day to absorb and explore this magical jewel of northern New Mexico.

With the namesake teepee-shaped formations set about like an encampment, you have a couple of hiking options to consider. There are two official trails: the 1.1-mile Cave Loop and the 1.3-mile Canyon Trail (one-way). Here, we'll start on the Cave Loop, soon connect to the Canyon Trail to explore up to the mesa top, and

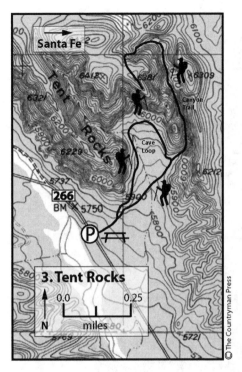

3. Tent Rocks

0.0   0.25

N   miles

© The Countryman Press

rattlesnakes, and jackrabbits. The trails throughout Tent Rocks are plenty wide, so avoid moving off-trail to help keep this resilient-but-fragile ecosystem unharmed. Tent Rocks also is known as Kasha-Katuwe, "white cliffs" in the traditional Keresan language of the local Pueblo people. Rocks, technically called boulder caps, balanced on hardened sand castle–like cones seem to defy gravity in many places along the hike.

At 0.5 mile along the Cave Loop trail you reach the cave itself. Set into the wall at the mouth of a tall slot canyon, a traditional pueblo ladder will put you at eye level with the small shelter. Past the cave the trail arches up to give you a view of the landscape leading back toward the trailhead. The mountain cluster you see in the distance is the Sandia Range, its highest point reaching 10,678 feet on the Sandia Crest. Tent Rocks is on Cochiti Pueblo land managed by the BLM and designated in 2001 as a national monument. Hollywood movies like *Lonesome Dove* and *Young Guns II* were filmed here.

The trail makes small dips and twists, connecting to the Canyon Trail at 0.8 mile. Head left for a fantastic journey into a narrow canyon and up to a highpoint with great vistas. To the right is the continuation of the Cave Loop, which travels 0.3 mile across the open zone back to the trailhead.

The mouth of the canyon is quite inviting, but as you reach deeper in, approximately 0.3 mile, you begin to feel the undulation of the canyon walls. It is as if they are breathing sandstone lungs, the exhales pinching the trail through narrow passages. The shaping of the rock is definitely a great wonder, done by tens of thousands of years of water and wind and the abrasive action of sand against the canyon walls. The trail twists through the

then rejoin the Cave Loop trail back to the trailhead.

A short distance down the Cave Loop trail to the left, you weave your way through a small cluster of tent rock formations. It will be tempting to run your fingers along the surface. Do so, but lightly, so as not to break loose any of the conglomerated materials. What you see today in this city of Turkish towers, or hoodoos, was originally a thick layer of ash, pumice, and tuff, at some points more than 1,000 feet deep, deposited from a series of volcanic eruptions that took place more than six to seven million years ago. Wind and water ate away at the soft layers to leave behind the tent rocks, canyons, and arroyos.

The area of Tent Rocks is a high desert zone home to plant species like yucca, juniper, Indian plume, and manzanita, as well as creatures like blue-tailed lizards,

Tent Rocks canyon

canyon like a mountain stream seeking the easiest path down. Nature is more into motion, contortions, odd leanings, and spirals than straight lines, and the walk through the canyon is a testament to this.

This hike does not involve canyoneering, technically speaking or otherwise, yet it does create a sensation similar to that experience, but without the element of danger. Heavy rains sometimes cause water to rush through here, though, making travel more difficult or ill-advised.

At 0.7 mile along the Canyon Trail you are in the upper canyon in a much wider zone, having lazily wound your way beneath some more amazing tent rock formations. A natural rock staircase marks the beginning of the short climb to the top of the mesa. It is 0.3 mile to the top, the trail climbing steeply the whole way. At one point you must make a ladder-like move over a rock. It is not overly difficult, but small children and those in poor physical shape may need some assistance.

Once you've topped out, there are a couple of trails to follow, the main one leading to a point that overlooks the Cave Loop area. Winds can be strong up here, especially on the point, so be mindful. Still,

it is a wonderful perch for taking in the immediate area, with additional views of all the major ranges in the area: the Jemez Mountains to the north, the Sangre de Cristos east-northeast, and the Sandia Mountains to the southeast. As tempting as it might be to seek an alternate route back to the trailhead from here, you must return the way you came because of the impassability of the terrain and the need to preserve the fragile features of Tent Rocks.

Cochiti Pueblo

Archeological finds have shown the present-day Cochiti Pueblo to have been continually inhabited since A.D. 1225, making it one of the oldest communities in North America. Research also has supported the idea that the Pueblo people of Frijoles Canyon were the ancestors of the Cochiti people. Most of the surrounding Pueblo people speak either Tewa or Towa (Tanoan languages), but the Cochiti people speak an unrelated language called Keresan. The Cochiti people farmed along the Rio Grande for more than 700 years. They also were excellent craftspeople who created beautiful pottery, and the tradition is still alive today.

4

Santa Fe Baldy Loop

Type: Pay or Overnight

Season: Late June to early October

Total distance: 16.9 miles

Rating: Moderate to strenuous

Elevation gain: 2,700 feet

Location: Pecos Wilderness, 13 miles northeast of Santa Fe

Maps: USGS Aspen Basin and Cowles

Getting There

Off Paseo de Peralta in Santa Fe, take Bishops Lodge Road north. At the first stoplight (0.2 mile), turn right onto Artist/Hyde Park Road, the road for Santa Fe Ski Basin. From here, it is 14.6 miles to the large parking area for the Winsor Trail and Santa Fe Ski Basin. There are out-houses at the trailhead.

The Trail

At 12,622 feet, Santa Fe Baldy is one of the premier highpoints of the southern Sangre de Cristo Mountains, and adding to the splendor of this classic northern New Mexico hike is the regal cirque situated at Lake Katherine. In autumn, the slopes leading up to the trailhead from Santa Fe and many points along this hike reveal brilliant golden-yellow pools of color floating above the green conifers—compliments of the thousands of acres of aspen trees.

The trail begins by diving into the trees, with a creek crossing immediately there-after. Next you begin climbing up switch-backs through a mixed forest of fir and aspen groves ringed by a carpet of green grasses and decorated with a fantastic collection of wildflowers. At 0.6 mile, with the more strenuous climbing behind, you reach a gate, a sign-in area, and the Ravens Ridge Trail junction.

Once through the gate you are officially in the Pecos Wilderness. The trail eases up along this stretch as you glide across a long gentle arc on the high west slope of the Rio Nambe drainage. You are still im-mersed in the forest, passing by lichen-covered rocks and crossing through patches of aspen that shimmer in yellow come the beginning of September.

At 0.8 mile you pass the junction for the

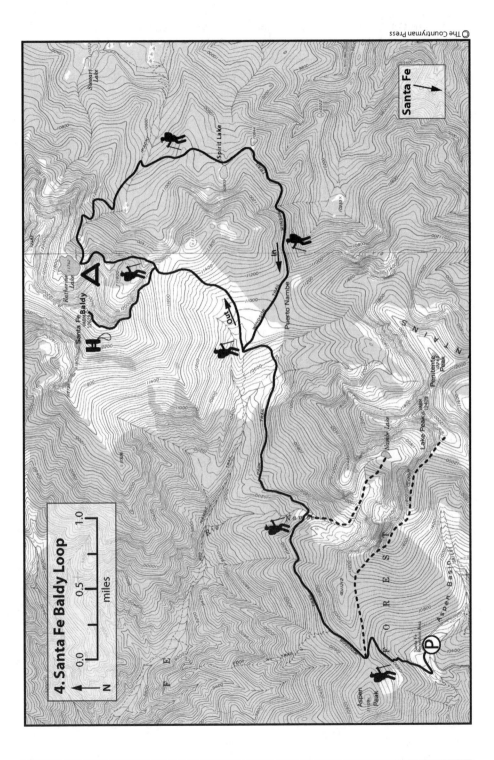

Rio Nambe Trail. And at 1.8 miles you reach a grassy open zone with views of a rocky basin to the south, as well as the infant Rio Nambe. This also is the junction for accessing Nambe Lake. Before you continue straight ahead to Santa Fe Baldy, take a break to absorb the scents of the forest and sounds of the creek. At 2.1 miles you pass the junction for the other end of the looping Rio Nambe Trail. The pleasant walk continues with an easy-going trail through mixed forest, with the added bonus of pocket meadows dotted with wildflowers. If you are paying attention and time it right, there are wild strawberries to be had, typically ripening around the end of July. There is also a nice glimpse of bare-topped Santa Fe Baldy at 2.3 miles.

The Sangre de Cristo Mountains of New Mexico are part of the southern Rocky Mountains, which extend into Colorado. In 1719, Spanish explorer Antonio Valverde y Cosio, noting the reddish hue of the high mountains at sunset, named the mountains the "Blood of Christ."

At 2.8 miles you cross a creek lined with globeflower and marsh marigold; past here the trail starts to climb. With the climbing, though, you also gain nice views of the surrounding landscape, including the Jemez Mountains to the west and Lake Peak (12,409 feet) and Penitente Peak (12,249 feet) in the near distance to the south, along with growing views of the shape and features of Santa Fe Baldy (12,622 feet) to the north.

You reach the Skyline Trail junction at 3.6 miles. It is set inside a broad, grassy, benched area lined with spruce trees, and when in bloom their cones have a noticeable raspberry color that complements the wildflower blooms growing in the meadow below. From the junction you take Skyline Trail 251, climbing through clusters of trees, and eventually above them, into a grass and rock zone that leads to a magnificent saddle at 4.9 miles. From here the trail climbs much more strenuously to gain the summit of Santa Fe Baldy. Continuing straight, the trail drops into the Lake Katherine basin and offers expansive views of the Pecos Wilderness.

It is a marvelous spin to the summit. The route is strenuous, but the exposed ridgeline trail snakes through wildflowers and a natural rock garden as it gains 1,000 feet. The beautiful scenery should keep you more than occupied with good thoughts. You'll reach a highpoint, but not the summit, at 1.3 miles. A short push 0.2 mile farther will have you standing on the windswept pinnacle of Santa Fe Baldy. As you would expect—and deserve after your efforts—the vistas are the best in the area, with a full view of the Jemez Mountains stretching from Abiquiu to Cochiti, the formidable cluster of the Truchas Peaks to the north, and the tree-choked expanse at the heart of the Pecos Wilderness to the east.

Even in the hottest days of summer it will be cool up here and the winds will ebb and flow from breezy to gale force depending on the threat of thunderstorms. Even in this harsh environment, the wildflowers are extremely vibrant, almost glowing—the bioluminescence of the subalpine and alpine—so be careful not to crush them. If you edge along the summit to the northeast you'll have an overlook of Lake Katherine nestled in a basin nearly 1,000 feet below.

To continue on to Lake Katherine, follow the trail back down the exposed ridge to the saddle and into the cover of trees, winding your way downslope to the southeast shoreline in 0.9 mile, or 8.8 miles total

Santa Fe Baldy

from the trailhead. The forest rims the southern end of the lake and the walls of the basin slide into the remaining shoreline, lush with grasses and wildflowers like columbine and alpine aven, which pop up en masse between and below craggy rock features. The lake is popular and has suffered somewhat due to the number of visitors that trample the understory near this end. Please be mindful. Northern New Mexico is in an extremely arid climate zone, so high-mountain lakes and the surrounding flora should be viewed as precious, fragile resources.

Near the east shoreline, close to the lake's outlet, is the continuation trail for looping back along a section of the Skyline Trail to rejoin the Winsor Trail and pass Spirit Lake. The trail from the lake loses el-

evation quickly, and at 0.3 mile (9.1 miles total) it passes by a water garden of sorts, a small, boulder-strewn tarn decorated with striated paintings created by rising and dropping watermarks. The trail shadows the course of the stream, which eventually becomes Winsor Creek, keeping you in a diverse riparian plant zone before it breaks off into a drier forest environment dominated by fir trees.

At 10.5 total miles you reach the junction with the Winsor Trail. Heading left would lead you to Stewart Lake in 1.2 miles. The trail to the right moves through the trees, crossing a creek and alternately gaining and losing elevation on the way to a small break where quaint and isolated Spirit Lake sits at 11.5 miles. The lake is for day use only and no campfires are allowed.

Moving on from Spirit Lake the trail gains some elevation, but in a very casual manner. It makes a high-slope run through the trees 2,000 feet above the Holy Ghost Creek drainage, but with breaks here and there that show glimpses of the Pecos Wilderness to the east. At 12.7 total miles you reach a signed junction marking the intersections of the Skyline Trail, a branch of the Skyline, and the Winsor Trail. Continue straight on the Winsor Trail, entering a forested bench area. Follow the pleasant course back to the junction with the Skyline Trail at 13.3 miles. From here it is 3.6 miles back to the trailhead, or 16.9 miles total.

Shooting the Skyline

No other trail in the Pecos Wilderness is adorned with as many natural splendors as the Skyline. The western end of the trail sits on 12,409-foot Lake Peak and the eastern end ceases near the Barillas Peak Lookout (9,362 feet), a distance of more than 60 miles. In between, this incredible scenic byway provides off-ramps to all the Pecos Wilderness giants, like Santa Fe Baldy, East Pecos Baldy, and the Truchas Peaks. The Skyline Trail also accesses backcountry gems like Horsethief Meadow, Rincon Bonito, Enchanted Lake, and Lost Lake.

5

Nambe Lake

Type: Day hike

Season: Late June to early October

Total distance: 5.6 miles

Rating: Moderate to strenuous

Elevation gain: 1,400 feet

Location: Pecos Wilderness, 13 miles northeast of Santa Fe

Maps: USGS Aspen Basin

Getting There

From Paseo de Peralta in S
Bishops Lodge Road north
stoplight (0.2 mile) turn right onto
Artist/Hyde Park Road, the access road
for Santa Fe Ski Basin. From here it is
14.6 miles to the large parking area for the
Winsor Trail and Santa Fe Ski Basin. There
are outhouses at the trailhead.

The Trail

In the Tewa language, *Nambe* means
"People of the Round Earth." Nambe Lake,
at 11,400 feet, is a major feeder for the
Rio Nambe, which flows down the western
slopes of the Sangre de Cristo Mountains
and along the Nambe Pueblo. It is believed
that before the early 1500s small villages
were scattered across the foothills below
Nambe Lake, providing the hunting and
gathering families access to the riches of
the river valley, as well as the game and
berries on the higher ground. Eventually
pueblo living was established in a fertile
zone along the Rio Nambe. This created
an agrarian society that, like other pueblos
of the greater Rio Grande corridor, was
eventually catholicized by the Spanish.

To reach the high mountain lake, follow
the Winsor Trail up through a mixed forest
of fir and aspen that is carpeted with
grasses and a diverse collection of wildflowers. At 0.6 mile you reach the Ravens
Ridge Trail junction, along with the sign-in
for the Pecos Wilderness Area. Lake Peak
(12,409 feet), accessed by the Ravens
Ridge Trail, is a worthy substitute for
the much more distant Santa Fe Baldy
(12,622 feet) when it comes to elevated
views of the surrounding area. It requires,
however, a similar strenuous push up to
the summit, much like the one you face in
reaching Nambe Lake.

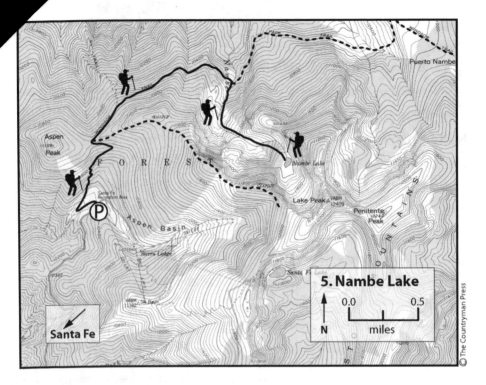

© The Countryman Press

5. Nambe Lake

0.0   0.5

N   miles

Santa Fe

You can first relax, though, because once through the gate the trail slides easily down through thick groves of aspen. After 1.8 miles of easy walking, you reach the trail junction for Nambe Lake. A complete change in scenery and challenge awaits you from this point forward. Gone are the aspen shimmer and the shadowy forest stroll, and in their place is a strenuous climb that parallels the lake's outlet, gaining serious chunks of elevation—1,000 feet—and offering open-air views of the twisted, steep-walled cirque that holds Nambe Lake.

In the beginning, you will see that the traffic of past human visitors has left behind an unnecessarily wide access trail, along with additional pathways most likely created during periods of receding snowpacks or when the trail was excessively wet. Drying out your hiking boots is far

easier than rebuilding a subalpine ecosystem, so be careful to keep your feet on the most traveled path. Doing so will allow surrounding areas to recover more quickly.

After you alternately grunt and rest over the 0.9-mile climb (2.7 miles total) the trail relents as it passes by a marshy area set in a narrow section of what feels like a hanging valley. An additional 0.1 mile brings you to small, clear Nambe Lake, set in a big cirque with tall, loose rock walls. The two highpoints some 600 vertical feet above the head of the basin are Lake Peak (known by the Nambe and Tesque Pueblos as Blue Stone Mountain) and Deception Peak (12,280 feet). As is the case with other cirque lakes of the Pecos Wilderness, wildflowers from marsh marigold to monkshood dot the lakeshore through the blooming season. Camping is not allowed in the Nambe Lake basin.

The Nambe Lake outlet

Splashing Through a Golden Sea

A fire in the late 1800s ravaged thousands of acres of the western slopes of the Sangre de Cristo Mountains above Santa Fe. The thick fir and spruce forest was destroyed, but more sun-loving tree species like aspen soon began to appear. These aspen still claim a staggering amount of mountainscape that, come autumn, shows in the crisp shimmer of the leaves, which range from sundrop yellow to fire orange. Aspen Vista, located along the ski basin road a few miles before the ski resort, is a wonderful but also wildly popular jump-off point into this aspen sea.

Atalaya Mountain

Type: Day hike

Season: April to October

Total distance: 6.6 miles

Rating: Strenuous

Elevation gain: 1,800 feet

Location: Santa Fe National Forest, on the eastern edge of Santa Fe

Maps: USGS Santa Fe and McClure Reservoir

Getting There

From Paseo de Peralta in Santa Fe, a couple of blocks east of the Plaza, turn left onto East Alameda. Drive 1.2 miles as the road bends over the Santa Fe River to Upper Canyon Road. Turn left onto Upper Canyon and drive 1.3 miles to the intersection with Cerro Gordo Road. Turn left—your only turn option—and then take the first right into the parking lot for the Dale Ball Trail System and Santa Fe Canyon Preserve.

The Trail

Beyond the dozens of art galleries along Canyon Road is this book's most relentless hike, Atalaya Mountain (9,121 feet). It shows itself from far below (1,800 vertical feet of climbing) in the rugged cliff face that overlooks the city of Santa Fe and the broad plateau that separates the Sangre de Cristos from the blue-tinged Jemez Mountains to the west. An early evening hike will have you twisting through blocks of pink quartzite and an evergreen forest of pinion pine up into crimson sunlight that reveals why the Sangre de Cristo Mountains were named "Blood of Christ" in Spanish.

Another badge of distinction for the Atalaya hike is the splendor of the trailhead location. The Santa Fe Canyon Preserve, which is accessed from the same parking area, hosts a huge variety of bird life feeding and living among the trees and plants. The trail system that loops the area should not be missed. An additional attribute of the Atalaya hike is the incredibly thorough trail-junction marking system present throughout the Dale Ball Trail System. Each junction is numbered and has a map indicating its location in respect to other junctions in the vicinity, as well as the distances between each. Getting lost here would be a real accomplishment.

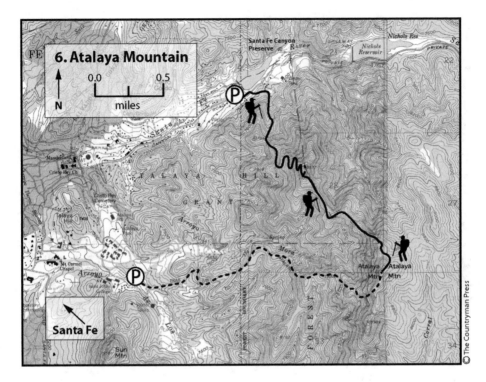

To begin, head through the gate at the opposite end of the parking lot, as if intending to wander through the preserve. Just past this fenceline another gate leads down into a swale and over the continuation of Upper Canyon Road to access the first section of trail up to Atalaya Mountain. The trail parallels the road overlooking the refuge before turning up a narrow ravine. Volcanic basalt and quartzite boulders litter the trailside as you climb up to the first of a half-dozen junctions at 0.7 mile.

The route continues to the left along the lower mid-slope of Picacho (8,577 feet). The local plant life consists of pinion pine, ponderosa pine, yucca, prickly pear cactus, and wildflowers like daisy and sunflower. At just before 1 mile you reach the second junction. Head left to start the corkscrew ascent of the steep west slope of Picacho. The views become bigger the higher you go.

By 1.9 miles you reach the short spur trail that takes you on to the summit of Picacho, with a high view over the preserve and out over the western slopes of the Sangre de Cristos below the Santa Fe Ski Basin. Stay straight to continue on one of the two trails heading for Atalaya. The spilt pathways meet up in less than 0.3 mile, the one to the left angling more directly cross slope and the right one making a few twisting bends that offer nice views of Atalaya.

The trail crosses a ridgeline saddle connecting the two highpoints, with a view down the beginning of Arroyo Mora to the west. At 2.7 miles you reach another junction, the fifth so far. Continue to the left, working along the arm and shoulder of Atalaya. The hiking is steep the whole way, but it really rockets straight up just beyond a cliff band around the 3-mile mark. By 3.3 miles you will be standing on the summit of

An arroyo near Atalaya Mountain

Atalaya, most likely catching your breath yet also taking in views of Santa Fe, mountainscapes of the Sandias and the Jemez Mountains, and close-ups of the lower slopes of the Sangre de Cristos.

It is possible to make this a through hike by continuing down the steep west slope of Atalaya and into the Arroyo de Los Chamisos, then on to the campus of St. Johns College. This route is approximately 4.5 miles. You would, of course, need to leave a vehicle on each end or be prepared to make the full loop along roads to return to the Dale Ball parking area, roughly 10.5 total miles.

Feeling Fowl?

It was only in the last six years that the Santa Fe Canyon Preserve (190 acres)

was nudged back into its natural state as a life-rich *bosque* fed by the Santa Fe River. Remnants of the original 1881 dam still can be seen. It retarded the river and began the decline of this amazing cottonwood and willow ecological zone, which today lures in bear, deer, the building talents of beaver, and more than 140 different species of bird life. A *bosque,* Spanish for "woodlands," is a low-lying zone (floodplain) where woodlands and riparian areas merge. Along the 1.5-mile interpretive trail, you can easily spot dozens of birds, from mallard or blue-winged teal to heron, western bluebird, and cedar waxwing. Find out more by visiting The Nature Conservancy web site at www.nature.org and linking to the preserve.

7

Truchas Peak (East)

Type: Overnight or multiday

Season: Late June to October

Total distance: 24.6 miles

Rating: Moderate to strenuous

Elevation gain: 4,750 feet

Location: Pecos Wilderness,
14 miles north of Pecos

Maps: USGS Cowles and Truchas Peak

Getting There

From the town of Pecos, take NM 63 north, which is also signed as Main Street. On the way out of town, you pass a sign reading TERRERO 14 MILES, COWLES 20 MILES. At 11.4 miles the road forks; the left one goes toward Holy Ghost and the right one toward Cowles. Take the right fork, which crosses the Pecos River and enters the community of Terrero. At 19.4 miles, you reach a left turn for the Panchuela Campground. (A large recreation sign also indicates the Cowles Campground to the left.) Cross the Pecos River and bear right shortly thereafter in the direction of the Panchuela Campground. You arrive at the parking lot and trailhead for this hike at 20.9 miles. There is a $2 per day, per vehicle fee; $5 per day for a campsite.

The Trail

Cloud-scraping peaks, high-elevation mountain lakes, open ridgeline traverses, creekside pathways, aspen-forested slopes, and sweeping vistas are all part of a multiday backpacking adventure at Truchas Peak (east). It strikes that sweet balance between hard work and the rewards of backcountry serenity. The massiveness of this zone of the Pecos Wilderness provides comfort and reminds us that we are part of nature's systems, not separate. Standing on top of New Mexico's second tallest mountain, Truchas Peak (13,102 feet), can make you feel both powerful and minuscule.

The more popular approach from the heart of the Pecos Wilderness up to Pecos Baldy Lake is along Jack's Trail. Starting out on Panchuela Creek and continuing with a spectacular mid-slope run along the Dockweiler Trail, however, makes the other approach just as worthy

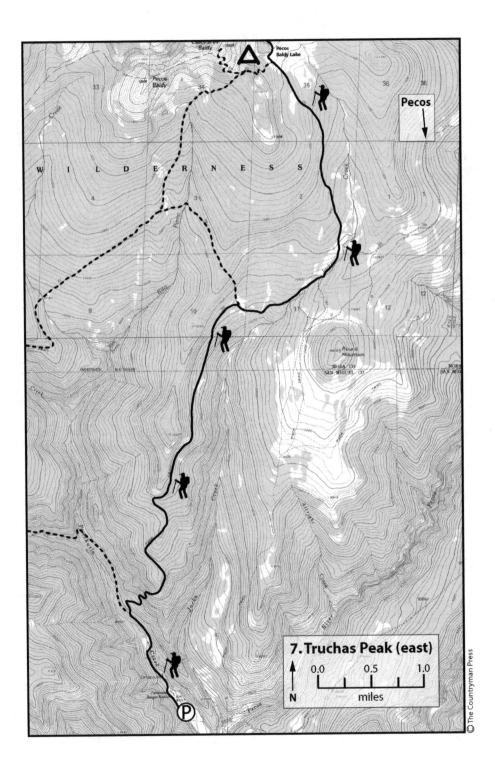

7. Truchas Peak (east)

0.0   0.5   1.0

N   miles

© The Countryman Press

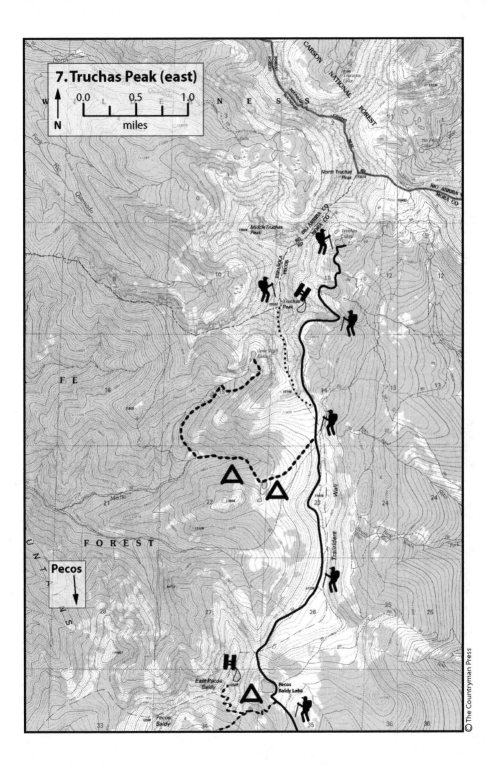

7. Truchas Peak (east)

© The Countryman Press

The view to North Trunchas Peak

and offers more solitude. For the latter, you slip through the picnic area below the parking lot to a footbridge to access the first section of trail. Panchuela Creek runs with a healthy volume of water through the summer, providing both melody and the nutrients for a diverse riparian ecosystem. The trail stays creekside for short pieces but mainly runs higher on the slope to the junction with the Dockweiler Trail at 0.7 mile. Doses of steeper climbing are part of the recipe for the next 2 miles before the trail eases up along a slope of ancient aspen. The first grind lasts about 0.7 mile as you switchback above the Panchuela Creek drainage and bend around to the head of the Jacks Creek drainage.

The trail moves through some aspen along a more relaxed ascent before climbing again at 1.8 miles, slipping into a predominantly fir forest. By 2.4 miles your hard work is rewarded by a beautiful aspen-dotted slope carpeted in lush grasses and wildflowers like iris and lupine. The trail moves above Jacks Creek with views to the opposite, equally aspen-rich slope and farther beyond to the green-grass corridor of Hamilton Mesa.

The junction with the Rito Perro Trail arrives within a big, open, grassy zone at about 4 miles. Popping into the trees and then out into a small meadow delivers you to the Jacks Creek Trail junction at 4.3 miles. You head left, or northeast, moving upstream for the next 0.6 mile before the trail veers away on a more northerly course. The route is set mainly in the trees with one nice meadow crossing, and you take out chunks of elevation by stair-stepping along a rocky and tree-rooted trail.

You next cross the outlet of Pecos Baldy Lake and enter an open slope shortly before reaching another trail junction at 6.3 miles. You need to head left at

the junction to reach Pecos Baldy Lake. Set below the east slope of East Pecos Baldy (12,529 feet), the small, round lake is an ideal home base for a day's exploration around the northwest section of the Pecos Wilderness. There are plenty of campsites up and off the lakeshore.

Once you have settled in at a campsite, your options are plentiful. You can reach the top of East Pecos Baldy by pushing up to a small saddle above the lake and then making a corkscrew ascent to the long summit, where the 360-degree vista spins from mountaintops to deep basins to blankets of forest. Another option, and the one you set out for originally on this hike, is the amazing promenade along the west side of a grassy mesa-like formation known as the Trailriders Wall, which feeds into the glacially shaped basins below the impressive Truchas Peaks triad.

To begin the Truchas approach, move around the northeast shoreline of Pecos Baldy toward a saddle about 150 vertical feet above and to the west of the lake. A whole new world opens up as you teeter above a huge basin and begin a 3-mile highline journey with growing views of the Truchas Peaks. The slope is a marvelous grassy playground that is a thrill in sunny weather, although it can feel a bit precarious when a thunderstorm is building. The nearest trees are a few hundred vertical feet below.

By 9.8 miles (the mileage is a continuation from Pecos Baldy Lake), you reach a collection of trail junctions. The first path to the left is an unmaintained trail that works down to a creekside run along the Rio Medio. The second left-side junction trail reaches the Rio Medio too, and also accesses Jose Vigil Lake, nestled in a steep and deep basin below the south slope of Truchas Peak and the Rio Quemado Trail.

The junction to the right provides access to a number of other trails, including Trail 257, which works its way back to Pecos Baldy Lake along the forested side of the Trailriders Wall.

This zone of junctions is a prime piece of real estate situated just beyond the north end of the Trailriders Wall, which comes up short in directly connecting East Pecos Baldy to the mountain string of the Truchas Peaks. From here you have two options depending on your objective. To gain the summit of Truchas Peak (13,102 feet) continue along the trail for about 0.2 mile before moving onto the shoulder ridgeline that is the southern approach to the top. There is an unofficial but discernable trail as you make your way higher, edging slightly to the west above the Jose Vigil Lake basin. From where the trail takes off it is about 1 mile to the summit, with an elevation gain of 1,400 vertical feet.

The summit of Truchas Peak is the most impressive of the high peaks in New Mexico. Gray rocky catwalks lead toward Middle Truchas Peak (13,066 feet) and North Truchas Peak (13,024 feet), as well as broad-shouldered Chimayosos Peak (12,841). The tightrope run could feasibly continue all the way to Jicarita Peak (12,835 feet) 8 miles to the northeast. Floating in the treed basin below and to the north are the Truchas Lakes. Virtually the whole Pecos Wilderness is at your feet, as is the Rio Grande valley as it slides into the Jemez Mountains. The Wheeler Peak Wilderness is faintly visible on the horizon to the north, and to the south are numerous highpoints along the backbone of the Sangre de Cristo Mountains.

Another option is to continue on the trail for 2.3 miles (12.3 miles total), bending in and out of the mini-basins below the steep east face of Truchas Peak. You move through white boulder fields while grabbing a handful or two of currants—ripe in September—on the journey up to the Truchas Lakes. The lakes are pressed against the 1,000-foot wall wrapping around from Truchas Peak to Chimayosos Peak and beyond, and the smaller one is stacked above the larger one. Below the lakes, a vein-like network of rivulets converges 1,000 feet below into the Rito de los Chimayosos, which eventually feeds the Pecos River near Beatty's Flats. No camping is allowed in the Truchas Lakes basin.

A Sea of Ice

New Mexico has a history—albeit one that ended some 70 million years ago—with the sea, still visible today in the numerous sedimentary rock layers and fossilized sea life visible all across northern New Mexico. It is difficult enough to imagine this region as home to sharks and clams and even great cypress forests along salty shorelines, but then try adding the fact that New Mexico was once encased in ice. The results of the melting or retreating glaciers, which occurred from 1.5 million to 15,000 years ago, are the U-shaped valleys and basins of the Pecos Wilderness, along with the sharp edges of the Truchas Peaks and the highpoints and ridgelines around Wheeler Peak.

8

Pecos Baldy Lake Loop

Type: Overnight or multiday

Season: Late June to October

Total distance: 16 miles

Rating: Moderate to strenuous

Elevation gain: 4,100 feet

Location: Pecos Wilderness,
14 miles north of Pecos

Maps: USGS Cowles and Truchas Peak

Getting There

From the town of Pecos, take NM 63 north, also signed as Main Street. On the way out of town you pass a sign reading TERRERO 14 MILES, COWLES 20 MILES. At 11.4 miles, the road forks. The left option is for Holy Ghost and the right for Cowles. Take the right fork, which crosses the Pecos River and enters the community of Terrero. At 19.4, miles you reach the left turn for the Panchuela Campground. (A large recreation sign also indicates Cowles Campground to the left.) Cross the Pecos River and bear to the right shortly thereafter in the direction of the Panchuela Campground. You reach the parking lot and trailhead for this hike at 20.9 miles. There is a $2 per day, per vehicle fee; $5 per day for a campsite.

The Trail

The terrain around East Pecos Baldy and Pecos Baldy Lake is by far the most dramatic in the realm between the subapline and alpine, and the vistas are as good as any you will encounter in northern New Mexico. The triad of Truchas Peaks to the northwest; the stunning promenade of the Trailriders Wall, which separates two incredible basins and connects East Pecos Baldy and the Truchas Peaks; and the treed and meadow-pocked Pecos Wilderness make this setting a backpacker's must. The approach is also enhanced by the flower-filled meadows, lush creekside flora and fauna, aspen-lit slope, and cave exploration.

From the parking lot, walk into the picnic area to reach a footbridge across Panchuela Creek. You will be creekside for a number of miles as you move along Panchuela Creek and then Cave Creek. The tree mix is fir and aspen, with an active

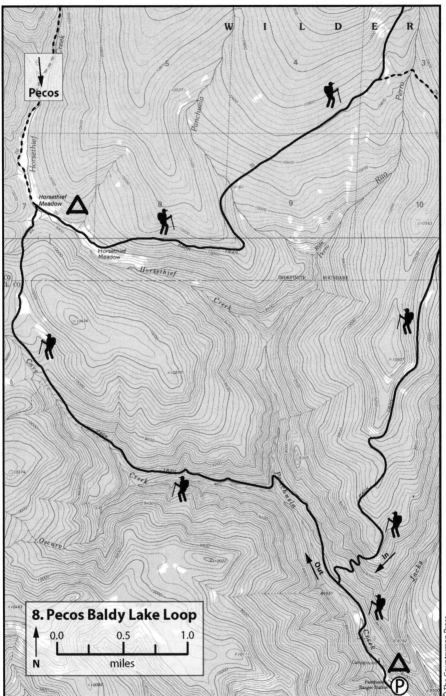

8. Pecos Baldy Lake Loop

0.0   0.5   1.0
N   miles

Pecos

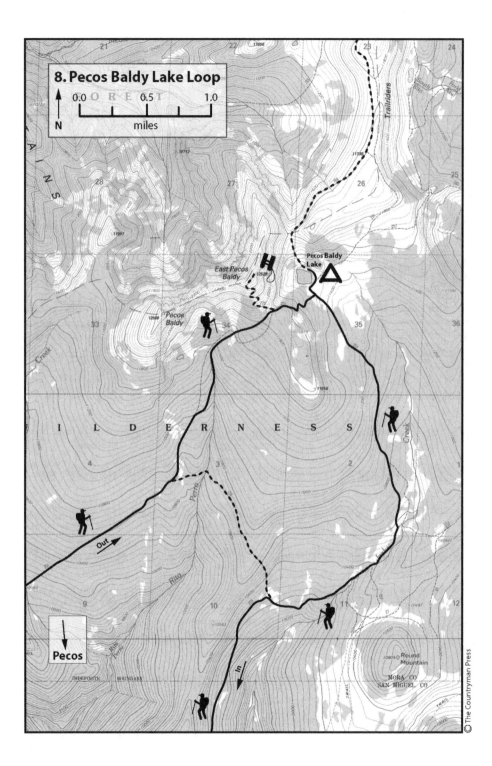

Summit view from East Pecos Baldy

understory of wild rose (whose fruit we know as the rosehip), blankets of green grasses, and a broad variety of wildflowers, from aster and daisy to yarrow, harebell, and paintbrush. The official entry into the Pecos Wilderness is marked with a sign around 0.4 mile.

The trail gains a bit of high ground above the creek shortly past the wilderness boundary. It moves through an open tree zone before reaching the junction with Dockweiler Trail 259 at 0.8 mile. You continue straight on what is signed as Dave Creek Trail 288. The trail slides back down along the creek at 1.1 miles, with another beautiful arrangement of wildflowers, including scarlet gilia, sunflowers, thistle, and wild strawberry. At 1.4 miles the trail slips over Panchuela Creek via a footlog

and enters the Cave Creek drainage. This drainage is a little tighter in the beginning, and it's more treed but still has very pleasant shades of green in the understory and splashes of color in the wildflowers. Keep your eye out because a number of caves can be accessed along this stretch. In fact, the creek flows right through a few. The trail stays creekside for a short distance before gaining elevation moderately.

By 2.6 miles the Cave Creek drainage begins to broaden, giving the trail a more open and airy feel as it gains elevation more steeply and then transitions to a rolling stair-step ascent. There is a view back down the tree-choked drainage, where Cave Creek slips down boulders and other obstructions in small, picturesque cascades. At 3.1 miles you reach the junction with Skyline Trail 251. Stay straight, continuing on the trail to Horsethief Meadow. The trail follows a small creek for about 0.3 mile before making a short, steep push up and away, leaving behind the sounds of rushing water that have been with you for more than 3 miles.

Ancient seas and the shrinking ice sheets did their part in shaping the upper Pecos landscape around this hike. Identifiable along Cave Creek and into Horsethief Meadow are extremely ancient sedimentary rocks—some 300 million years old—as well as bluffs of granite from the Precambrian era—the oldest geologic period.

If conditions are right, there will be numerous varieties of mushrooms, including edible kinds like boletus and chanterelles, along this stretch of forest. You pass through a small meadow before beginning to lose elevation in the approach to Horsethief Meadow at 4.4 miles. Horsethief is a beautiful meadow that runs for about 0.75 mile. Tall grasses, wildflowers, and Horsethief Creek make this an excellent camping spot. Indian artifacts dating from hundreds of years ago have been found in the area. The meadow's name comes from tales of stolen horses being brought here and run out in the meadow for a time, then rebranded and moved out westward across the Sangre de Cristos. The trail, marked with a sign for Pecos Lake, makes a relaxing run across most of the meadow, the edges torched with yellow aspen in the fall.

Aspens also light up the slopes across the way, and you encounter small sections of tree shade before sliding back into a more consistent forest environment at 4.9 miles. You gain elevation until 5.7 miles, where there is a slight drop to a crossing of Panchuela Creek at 6 miles. Panchuela's headwaters are about 2 miles

north of here, below the lower west slope of Pecos Baldy. The Pecos Wilderness contains somewhere in the neighborhood of 150 miles of streams and 28 lakes.

The trail crosses the creek and continues up and down on a cross-slope run along the Rito Perro drainage. At 7.3 miles you reach the junction with Rito Perro Trail 256 in a nice open zone that provides views of Pecos Baldy (12,500 feet). Head to the left crossing through the open area and on into a creek-fed ravine at 8.2 miles. This is the steepest, most strenuous section of the hike to this point, as you gain about 1,200 vertical feet in less than 2 miles. The trail crosses into a basin of sorts below the east slopes of Pecos Baldy before reaching the junction with the trail to the summit of East Pecos Baldy at 9.1 miles. This junction is set in an open zone/saddle with a great overlook of Pecos Baldy Lake.

The summit trail is 1 mile long and gains 800 vertical feet, zigzagging up the east slope to reach the long, bench-like peak of East Pecos Baldy (12,529 feet) and vistas galore. The most prominent views are of the Trailriders Wall just below and to the north. It runs into the signature peaks of the Pecos Wilderness in Truchas Peak (13,102 feet), Middle Truchas (13,066 feet), and North Truchas (13,024 feet). To the east-southeast, the long, open, green corridor is Hamilton Mesa. To the south you will see Redondo Peak and Santa Fe Baldy. The views are indeed big, as you see across so much of the Pecos Wilderness from here—all the gentle high valleys, steep creek drainages, and deep basins.

Bypassing the trail to the summit of East Pecos Baldy, the trail works downslope to the lake in less than 0.3 mile (9.4 miles). The lake presses up against the sheer walls of East Pecos Baldy's north face, while the opposite shoreline welcomes a seemingly boundless stretch of forest and high open valleys to the north. There is a very relaxing feeling up here, with plenty of campsites up and off the shoreline. There also are plenty of opportunities for day hikes around Trailriders Wall, a summit outing to one of the glacially shaped Truchas Peaks, or various other explorations.

Looping back, the trail drops from here along Jacks Creek Trail 257, crossing an open slope and over the outlet for Pecos Baldy Lake before slipping into a forest. It is a mix of moderate and steeper descents along a rocky and tree-rooted trail at points. You pass through a forest of fir and aspen, with a slopeside meadow coming at 10.2 miles and the junction with the Dockweiler Trail 259 (northbound) at 11.1 miles. Continue on the Jacks Creek Trail, actually along the creek itself, for another 0.6 mile to reach the Dockweiler Trail junction to the south. Pass through a small meadow, duck into the trees, and pop back out onto a big open grassy slope to reach the Rito Perro Trail junction at 12 miles.

The sensational slopeside garden of iris and lupine continues as the trail contours along the drainage and slips between ma-jestic aspen groves. You have views across to a similar slope of open meadow and aspen, as well as slivered views of Hamilton Mesa farther to the east. By 13.6 miles, the trail drops a little more steeply and enters a fir-dominated forest. It relaxes a bit after winding downslope at around 14.2 miles and then reenters the aspen zone, but with a sparse understory. At 14.6 miles the trail takes another steeper fall via some switchbacks as you make your way back into the Panchuela Creek drainage. The junction with the Dave's Creek Trail arrives at 15.3 miles. Another 0.7 mile or so and you are back at the trailhead (16 miles total).

I'm Sticking with Jack

Most backpackers looking to access Pecos Baldy Lake leave from the Jacks Creek trailhead located at the end of FS 555. (Instead of turning left for Panchuela Campground, continue straight to reach this trailhead.) The trail follows high along the east side of the Jacks Creek drainage, passing underneath Round Mountain (10,809 feet) before reaching the Dockweiler Trail junction and continuing up to the lake along the same route as the hike described above. The round trip for this hike is 14 miles.

9

Apache Canyon to Glorieta Baldy

Type: Day hike

Season: June to October

Total distance: 9 miles

Rating: Moderate to strenuous

Elevation gain: 2,400 feet

Location: Santa Fe National Forest, 9 miles east-southeast of Santa Fe

Maps: USGS Glorieta and McClure Reservoir

Getting There

From Paseo de Peralta in downtown Santa Fe, take Old Santa Fe Trail Road south. In approximately 0.3 mile, turn left to stay on Old Santa Fe Trail Road (continuing straight would put you on Old Pecos Trail Road). Old Santa Fe Trail Road also is known as CR 67. At 8 miles, you bear left onto Canada Village Road (Old Santa Fe Trail Road continues straight). Pass through Canada Village, where the road surface transitions from pavement to packed dirt (8.8 miles). At 10.2 miles, take the left fork onto FR 79 at the sign for the Santa Fe National Forest. The parking area for this hike is at 12.9 miles. Follow the road to the right to begin hiking.

The Trail

Glorieta Baldy offers the finest overview of the Pecos Wilderness and Galisteo Basin of any highpoint in the area. Throw in an approach that moves through a portion of Apache Canyon's majestic trees and also across fantastic subalpine slopes and ridges and you have one of the most challenging and memorable outings in the Santa Fe area.

After following the road from the parking area for 0.3 mile you pass through a gate and arrive at the official trailhead. There is a trail marker for Baldy Trail 175 and a sign that shows the route to Glorieta Baldy and explains how this trail came to be. The trail was created, with support from the forest service, in memory of Otto Gruninger, who loved these mountains. The trail moves along a ridge that provides views over Santa Fe and across the Pajarito Plateau before bending downslope to meet a logging road at 0.7 mile. A small arrow indicates that the route continues to the left. Follow the bending road for an-

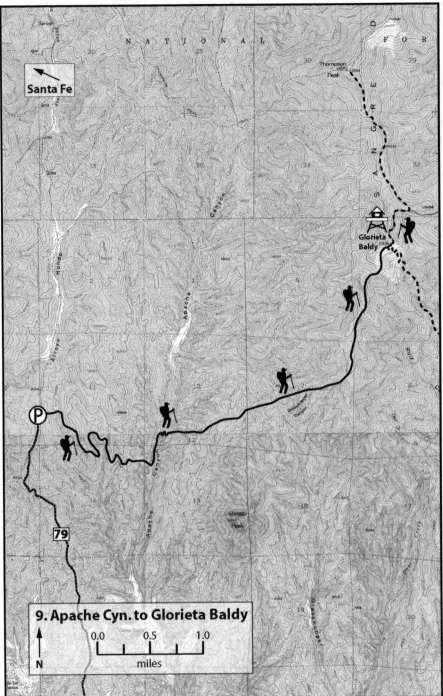

9. Apache Cyn. to Glorieta Baldy

0.0   0.5   1.0

miles

N

© The Countryman Press

other 0.7 mile to a trail junction. This area is a blend of life zones, combining high plateau plants like yucca, pinion pine, and juniper with low-level subalpine flora like Gamble oak and ponderosa pine.

A small sign indicates that the path to the right heads to Glorieta Baldy on Baldy Trail 175. The trail drops into Apache Canyon, with views of Shaggy Peak (8,847 feet) across the way and then up the canyon itself. A marvelous natural arboretum is located along the canyon floor. Apache Creek is the life force nurturing a diverse mix of old and massive fir, pine, spruce, cottonwood, juniper, and aspen—definitely a rare treat for northern New Mexico. At 1.2 miles you reach another trail junction. Head right, or upslope, on the trail signed for Glorieta Baldy. An information sign here highlights the importance and interconnected nature of the Galisteo Creek watershed.

Once out of the canyon, the trail topography alternates between short climbs and ridge runs. By 2.5 miles you are high enough to enjoy views down Apache Canyon, to Shaggy Peak now below you, and to the expanse of Galisteo Basin. The trail climbs steeply through a ponderosa pine forest before easing up as it gains the southern ridgeline leading to Glorieta Baldy at 3.4 miles. It's smooth going from here as the trail moves across the ridgetop through fir and aspen trees, only climbing a little. Your first good view of the Glorieta Baldy lookout comes at 4.3 miles.

Shortly beyond this point you pass by Trail 272, which accesses the Glorieta Conference Center (5 miles one-way). The old lookout site, built in 1940, is reached at 4.5 miles. The views from Glorieta Baldy are nice from the ground but spectacular from the lookout, with picture-perfect looks toward the Truchas Peaks to the north and Galisteo Basin to the south. Unfortunately, the lookout is currently closed due to lack of maintenance.

Galisteo Basin Preserve

A new and progressive model that combines conservation, restoration, and development is under way in the central zone of the Galisteo Basin, just outside the town of Lamy. When completed, there will be some 30 miles of hiking and riding trails, and a riparian restoration project will have invigorated 12 miles of habitat to the benefit of animal and plant species. Also, a 300-unit housing development will exist within this 12,800-acre preserve. Spearheaded by the Commonweal Conservancy, the project was born out of the desire to keep the former ranch site from being subdivided into multiple lots for private development. To learn more, visit www.galisteobasinpreserve.com.

10

Glorieta Canyon

Type: Day hike

Season: June to October

Total distance: 6.6 miles

Rating: Moderate

Elevation gain: 900 feet

Location: Santa Fe National Forest, 12 miles east-southeast of Santa Fe

Maps: USGS Glorieta and McClure Reservoir

Getting There

From Santa Fe, travel 16 miles southeast on I-25 to Exit 299, which is the first exit for Pecos and the access to Glorieta. Cross back over the interstate and turn left toward the Glorieta Conference Center. It is 0.6 mile to the conference center gate. Pass through the gate and stay to the right, ringing the center of the conference grounds. In 0.2 mile, you reach Oak Street. Turn right here to continue to the hiker's parking area for Glorieta Canyon (16.9 miles).

The Trail

The name Glorieta in this region is most associated with Glorieta Pass, the gateway between the Southwest and the Great Plains. For hundreds of years, tribes and Pueblo people passed through the canyon opening, located a few miles to the southwest of Glorieta Canyon, to trade with one another. The Spanish followed in the 1500s, and by the mid-1800s the Santa Fe Trail was a well-established trade route, as well as the "highway" for those looking to discover the Wild West. Glorieta Canyon's human history is marked by the remnants of a lumber mill and the foundation of a hotel. Once a place of commerce, it is now known as the Ghost Town.

About 30 yards past the parking area you follow a paved road up to the RV parking area, which is just over 0.1 mile. There is a hiking registry at the entrance to this parking area. To reach the actual trail, continue through the long parking area to a gate at the northwest end. The trail from here is actually the old road that accessed the lumber mill up the canyon. The mill planed its last board in the early 20th century. The roadway becomes more like a trail the farther up the canyon you travel.

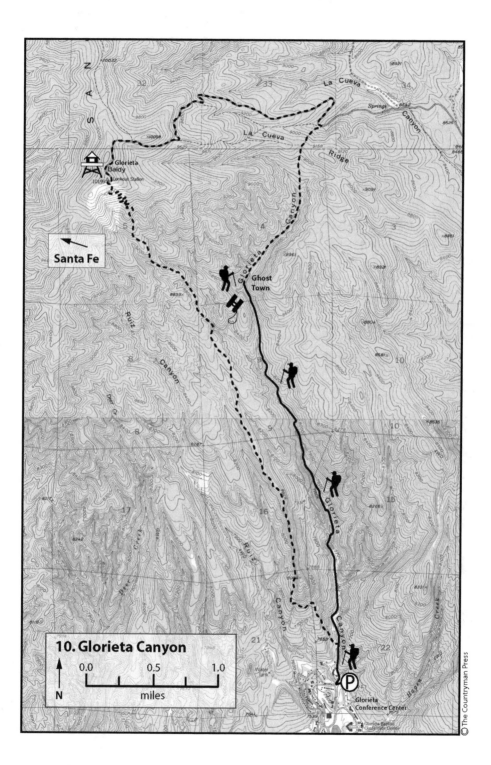

A rusting car body along Glorieta Creek

The initial setting is an open forest with a mix of Gamble oak and pine trees. As you follow Glorieta Creek past a horse corral 0.3 mile up from the RV parking lot, you walk through a gate into a more open zone littered here and there with attempts at human ingenuity. Next you enter a more wooded zone that is lined with wildflowers from late spring into summer. Aspen trees also are sprinkled about through here, lighting the pathway in autumn.

By 1.2 miles you reach a landmark from the past, an old 1930s-era truck seemingly sinking back into the ground, dispersing all the natural resources from which it was created back to the earth. Spiders have spun nests in the numerous cavities of the vehicle, much like they would in downed and hollowed trees. By 2.3 miles the forest adds more spruce and fir and the trail cuts slightly uphill above the creek. The route is still nicely shaded, making it a welcome retreat on the hotter days of summer. You eventually dip back down along the creek.

At 3.3 miles you reach the old mill site. A dilapidated bridge and another shell of a vehicle welcome you to a large clearing. A sign marks this spot as the mill site. A decent-sized slash pile sits on the east side of the clearing like an oversized beaver dam. In another 0.2 mile you reach the old hotel site, still recognizable by its foundation and the crumbling wood beams that once held up the multiroom guest resi-dence. Continuing on this trail you reach a road and a trail that leads, with some effort of course, to the top of Glorieta Baldy (10,199 feet) in 4 miles. This peak can also be reached by an alternate trail that leaves from the same end of the parking area and heads up Ruiz Canyon. It is an 11-mile trip that gains nearly 3,000 vertical feet to reach the summit, an old fire lookout, and brilliant vistas down the Pecos River canyon, across the Pecos Wilderness, and out over the Galisteo Basin.

War Zone

Numerous conflicts have taken place over the centuries in the vicinity of Glorieta, but the one best remembered today occurred at the Glorieta Battlefield. At the end of March 1862, a multiday Civil War battle commenced when regulars from Fort Union and a group of Colorado volunteers tried to halt the advance of Texas Confederates led by Brigadier General Henry H. Sibley. The Confederates already had taken Albuquerque and Santa Fe and were bound for the gold fields of Colorado, hoping to eventually control the whole Southwest all the way on the Pacific Ocean. Sibley's army was far superior in battle and had victory well in sight, but he signed a truce after only a few days of fighting upon learning that his ill-protected supply train had been completely destroyed by Union soldiers.

11

Pecos Ruins

Type: Day hike

Season: Year-round

Total distance: 1 mile

Rating: Easy

Elevation gain: 35 feet

Location: Pecos National Historic Park, 10 miles southeast of Santa Fe

Maps: USGS Pecos

Getting There

From Santa Fe travel 16 miles southeast on I-25 to Exit 299, which is the first exit for Pecos and the access for Glorieta. Cross back over the interstate and look for signs directing you to the Pecos National Historic Park on the right. Approximately 6 miles down NM 50, turn right at a stop sign in the town of Pecos. There are signs again for the monument. After another 1.7 miles, you will see a sign on the right for the visitor center and park entrance. The parking area and visitor center are reached in 0.2 mile (23.9 miles total).

The Trail

There was a time, not so long ago, that the Pecos people thrived in this area thanks to a well-established agricultural system and the trade that took place between area Pueblo farmers and Plains tribes. They exchanged items like pottery and textiles for buffalo hides and shells. This was also a place of bloodshed between Indian peoples, and later the Spanish. Going back even farther, this area has had some kind of human presence for nearly 10,000 years, and small communities still exist here today. The Pecos Ruins embody what archeologists term the Rio Grande Classic Period (A.D. 1325–1600) and later the Spanish (A.D. 1540–1840).

The visitor center is well worth your time, as Pecos can be appreciated far more with a degree of historical context. The Pecos Pueblo and its incarnations under Spanish control, as well as that of the Union Army, have been of great significance to many cultures over different periods here. Physically the pueblo lies in the Pecos River valley, guarded to the south by the Glorieta Mesa and to the north by the Pecos Wilderness, which flows like green

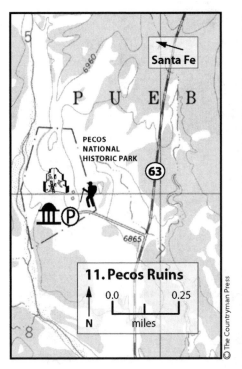

© The Countryman Press

11. Pecos Ruins

0.0   0.25

N   miles

Santa Fe

P U E B

PECOS
NATIONAL
HISTORIC PARK

63

6865

lava from the Sangre de Cristo high peaks, painted with winter snows well into June.

Water was much more readily available in the days of the active pueblo, originating from the high mountain snowpacks and running by the small rise, or mesa, upon which the bulk of the accessible ruins are built. To add to their water supply, the native people built check dams to catch rain runoff and irrigate their fields of beans, corn, and squash. Geologically speaking, the southern terminus of the Sangre de Cristos, the long wall of Glorieta Mesa, and the Tocolote Range meet to create a small gap at Glorieta Pass to the west. The Glorieta-Pecos Corridor runs east and then south, cut through an ancient seabed by the Pecos River over millions of years.

An easy-going gravel path loops by a number of pueblo and Spanish ruins. An interpretive guide, available at the visitor center, helps provide context. The loop first takes you by an open field that once held crops. It also was a campground for the buffalo hide tipis of trading Plains people. You will have two perspectives on the mission, built in 1717, the first coming from below. The structure is a combination of original and restored adobe bricks. "Original" is only true to a point, though, because what stands here is a much smaller and newer version of a church built in the 1620s. The first church was destroyed by the Pecos people in the Pueblo revolts of 1680, which took place in many locations across northern New Mexico.

The loop continues past an accessible kiva, the south and north Pueblo ruins, and the ruins around the church. The North Pueblo ruins were, in their time, an incredibly well-conceived, well-built structure that reached heights of five stories and contained some 600 rooms connected by porches on the upper levels. It had a fortress-like feel due to its defensive design and its location on the highpoint of the area. Construction began in the 1400s and the structure was occupied for 200 years.

The area where the decaying church stands is called the Mission Complex. The first church was much bigger than the one standing here today. It stretched some 150 feet in length and its series of exterior buttresses and six bell towers were said to have included 300,000 adobe bricks weighing 40 pounds each. The other buildings and structures you see served as living quarters, classrooms, kitchen, dining room, and stables. There also was a garden. The kiva in the middle of the ruins was built during the Pueblo revolt as an act of defiance. When the second church was built, this kiva was buried.

The Pecos National Historic Park occu-

The Pecos Ruins

pies three separate sections in the surrounding area. Public access is not allowed in areas beyond the Pueblo and mission ruins, both because excavation of other ruins continues and to respect the sacred land of the Pecos people. (This also includes the Glorieta Battlefield, which is accessible by guided tour only.) The Pecos Ruins are set in a high plateau zone of tall grasses, juniper, cactus, rain-coaxed wildflowers, and rattlesnakes, and there is a healthy community of local and migratory bird species.

Rest Stop, Theme Park, and Trailside Diner

During the 60-some years when the Santa Fe Trail experienced heavy use for commerce and migration, the Pecos Pueblo was used as a campsite, a place to replenish resources, and as an amusement park. Tales even were spun early on that the Aztec emperor Montezuma had resided here, which, of course, would have upped the ticket price if someone had been charging for a walk through the ruins. The Pecos people abandoned the pueblo by the late 1830s, so there was no one left to explain its history from the standpoint of both the Indians and the Spanish. Wood beams from the mission were pilfered in the 1850s to build houses and other outbuildings on the Kozlowski Ranch, now part of the park. It was a desired meal stop for passing stagecoaches.

Hamilton Mesa

Type: Day hike

Season: Late June to October

Total distance: 10.1 miles

Rating: Moderate

Elevation gain: 850 feet

*Location: Pecos Wilderness,
19 miles north of Pecos*

*Maps: USGS Elk Mountain and
Pecos Falls*

Getting There

From Pecos, take NM 63 north. At 11.4 miles, the road forks. The left option is for Holy Ghost and the right for Cowles. Take the right fork, which crosses the Pecos River and enters the community of Terrero. You reach the right turn for FS 223 at 18 miles. This is the road for the Iron Gate Campground, and it's rough and rutted. A high-clearance, four-wheel-drive vehicle is recommended. You arrive at the parking area and small campground at 22 miles. There is a $2 per day, per vehicle fee; $5 per day for a campsite.

The Trail

Hamilton Mesa is an anomaly in a wilderness already filled with spectacularly unique geographic features. This Pecos Wilderness darling defies the encroachment of trees, maintaining its open, long grassy swath. It is a magnificent parkland for idle strolling on a grand scale, with wildflowers decorating the ground and regal mountains silhouetted against the big northern New Mexico sky. The Hamilton Mesa Trail stretches beyond the signature portion of the mesa an additional 4 miles to provide access to deeper backcountry locations like Pecos Falls or the rarely visited collection of high lakes in Santiago, Pacheco, and Enchanted.

From the campground, the trail moves through a wide-spaced forest zone and winds its way to the junction with Trail 240 at 0.3 mile. You continue north, heading left on the Hamilton Mesa Trail. The openness continues in the form of a long overlook across the Rio Mora valley. The next junction comes with Rociada Trail 250 at 0.8 mile. The Rociada descends Hamilton Mesa's east slope to reach Mora Flats.

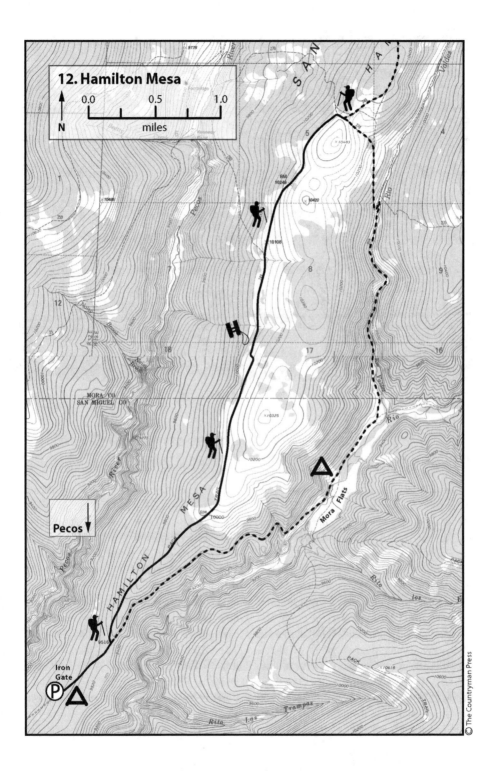

12. Hamilton Mesa

0.0   0.5   1.0

miles

N

Pecos

Mora Flats

HAMILTON   MESA

Iron
Gate

© The Countryman Press

The hike to Hamilton Mesa takes you past a variety of wildflowers.

Compared to the rewards, the work ahead is really nothing, however, there is some elevation to be gained. The trail climbs moderately across rocks and tree roots to a stock gate at 1.5 miles. Through the gate a slightly more rigorous ascent awaits, but so too do higher views across the Rio Mora valley. You'll have a front row seat for the mountainous backbone of the Pecos, anchored by Teseque Peak (12,043 feet) in the south and capped by Jicarita Peak (12,835 feet) to the north. The anticipation builds as the trail flattens out and edges along a thick grove of aspen and the peaks are unveiled one at a time, starting with summit views of Santa Fe Baldy (12,622 feet) and more full views of Redondo Peak (12,357 feet) and eventually Pecos Baldy (12,500 feet), East Pecos Baldy (12,529 feet), and the 13,000-foot triplets in Truchas, Middle Truchas, and North Truchas.

The stroll through here is magnificent as all these peaks—including Chimayosos Peak (12,841 feet), the nearby and impressive neighbor to North Truchas—stay in sight for nearly 2 miles. In addition, colorful wildflowers like iris, paintbrush, cinquefoil, and bluebells do their best to steal your attention throughout the summer. By 3.5 miles, after a few very brief sections of trees, you reach the Larkspur Trail 260 junction. This trail descends into the Pecos River valley and accesses Beatty's Flats. In 1990 the Pecos River, from its headwaters in an unnamed basin south of Rincon Bonito to the town of Terrero, was protected as a Wild and Scenic

River. To qualify, rivers must be free of man-made obstructions and have an untouched ecosystem along their banks.

The geographical treats and amazing flora continue for another 1.2 miles (4.7 miles total) before the Hamilton Mesa Trail enters a forested environment. For day-trippers this signals the end of the journey, but for those seeking deeper backcountry it is 3.2 miles to the trail junction for Pecos Falls and an additional 1.2 miles to the Gascon Trail, which connects with the Skyline Trail to access Santiago Lake and the cross-country-only treks to Pacheco and Enchanted Lakes.

"Place Where There Is Water"

The Keresan Indian translation for the Spanish word *pecos* is "place where there is water." We see the word repeatedly in this region—Pecos Pueblo, Pecos River, Pecos Wilderness. The Pecos Wilderness was part of the first wave of wilderness designations in 1964. The state's second largest wilderness area, at 223,667 acres, it is the heart of backcountry adventures in northern New Mexico. It contains 445 miles of trails that lead to amazing settings like Hamilton Mesa, Santa Fe Baldy, Truchas Lakes, Trampas Lakes, Rincon Bonito, Pecos Falls, and Hermit Peak. The easy-traveling roads to the trailheads also make this area popular. And in a region that is poor in water, the Pecos has more than 100 miles of creeks and rivers, along with 28 lakes.

13

Mora Flats to Hamilton Mesa Loop

Type: Day hike

Season: Late June to October

Total distance: 10.1 miles

Rating: Moderate

Elevation gain: 1,200 feet

Location: Pecos Wilderness, 19 miles north of Pecos

Maps: USGS Cowles, Elk Mountain, and Pecos Falls

Getting There

From Pecos, take NM 63 north. At 11.4 miles, the road forks. The left option is for Holy Ghost and the right for Cowles. Take the right fork, which crosses the Pecos River and enters the community of Terrero. You reach the right turn for FS 223 at 18 miles. This is the road for the Iron Gate Campground, and it's rough and rutted; a high-clearance, four-wheel-drive vehicle is recommended. The parking area and small campground are at 22 miles. There is a $2 per day, per vehicle fee; $5 per day for a campsite.

The Trail

This hike is a beautiful mix of wide-spaced forest settings, grassy meadows, and creek corridors, capped off by the spectacular open run of Hamilton Mesa—a natural runway to the most dramatic peaks of the Pecos Wilderness. In the height of the wildflower season, especially when the early summer explosion of iris occurs, it will be a struggle to decide whether to scan the natural beauty of the flora or revel in the geological artwork above and beyond the Pecos River valley.

From the parking area, the trail winds through the trees to a junction with Trail 240 at 0.3 mile. Head left, continuing on Hamilton Mesa Trail 249, and begin a canyon-rim stroll above the Rio Mora valley to the junction with Rociada Trail 250. Follow this trail as it takes its time losing elevation to eventually reach the Rio Mora valley and Mora Flats. In the process you are treated to slopes covered in grass and wildflowers in summer, and displaying the yellow shimmer of aspen in the fall. Other plant and tree species include wild rose, ground juniper, oak and fir trees, and a small collection of stately ponderosa pines.

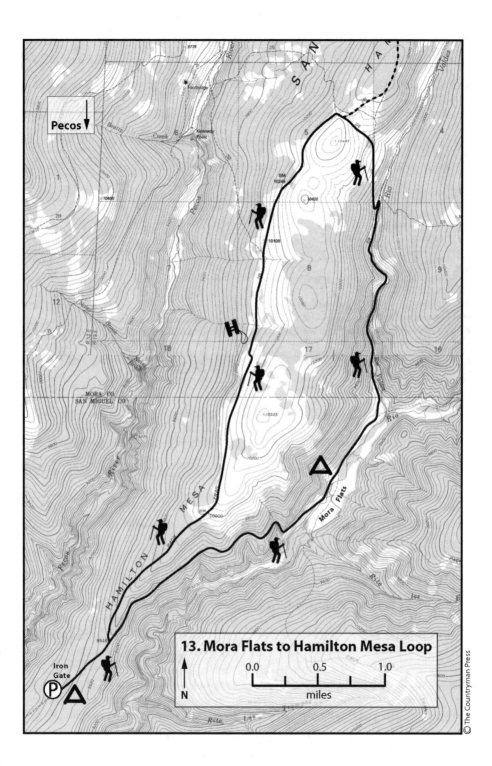

13. Mora Flats to Hamilton Mesa Loop

Columbine in bloom

The dead stand of trees across the valley and up the Rito los Esteros drainage is the result of a past wildfire. By 2.4 miles (1.6 miles down the Rociada Trail) you reach an overlook of Mora Flats and the Mora Canyon. Mora Flats stretches for approximately 1.5 miles, etched by the Rio Mora and decorated with clumps of grasses and wildflowers. Mora Flats is a boggy zone, but if you followed the creek downstream, you would eventually enter a deep, narrow gorge.

From here the trail quickly loses elevation on the way to the junction with Los Trampas Trail 240 and the entryway into Mora Flats (2.7 miles). You have to ford the river to reach Mora Flats. Stay straight to continue the loop, passing by a number of campsites on what can be a boggy section

of trail. You remain in an open corridor up to the junction with Valdez Trail 224 (3.2 miles) and for a short while longer as you work your way up the Rio Valdez valley.

The Valdez Trail slips into greater tree cover and edges along the Rio Valdez on a more rugged trail for 1.2 miles. There are a number of creek crossings as the drainage constricts, the first at 3.6 miles with three others following shortly. Take your socks off through here or wear some water sandals. At 4.5 miles you reach the junction with Bob Grounds Trail 270. Follow this trail on an immediate zigzag course upslope through a brief barrier of trees to a clearing. Around 0.2 mile up (4.7 miles total), the trail splits. Stay left, continuing up along a tree line until the trail cuts hard to the left, the direction you just came from while working up the Rio Valdez drainage.

Because of the lack of foot traffic and trail markers and the well-defined and distracting cow paths, it is easy to get off course through here. The trail follows the tree line but stays out in the open for less than 0.2 mile before making a switchback upslope. If you lose the trail look for the prominent ravine, which should contain running water, even late into summer. On the top of this ravine you will spot a cattle trough and the trail heading to the top of Hamilton Mesa, with its amazing views of the string of high summits to the west and north. The unmarked junction with the Hamilton Mesa Trail comes at 5.4 miles. This point is recognizable by the nearby stand of trees along the trail heading north. However, you need to take the trail to the left, or south.

The silent giants that follow you for a number of miles are the three 13,000-foot Truchas Peaks, East Pecos Baldy (12,529 feet), Pecos Baldy (12,500 feet), and Redondo Peak (12,357 feet). Hamilton Mesa is a marvelous treat, offering open views in all directions and a long canvas of wildflowers in the summer months. You pass the Larkspur Trail 260 junction at 6.6 miles. The walking so far has been easy, with relatively flat terrain that even de-

scends slightly at times. Past the junction, the trail crosses through a stand of trees and then pops back out into the open, continuing its very pleasant journey. By 7.8 miles the open feeling is still there, but views back up toward highpoints like the Truchas Peaks are obstructed by a stand of aspen.

There are views to the east over the Rio Mora valley and to other highpoints and valleys to the south. You pass through a stock gate at about 8.6 miles and make a steeper and rougher descent to the junction with Trail 250 (9.3 miles). From here you rejoin the same stretch you came in on to reach the trailhead at 10.1 miles.

Falls Flat

Hamilton Mesa is one of a few trails that will lead you to Beatty's Flats and Pecos Falls. Located 6 miles from Iron Gate, Beatty's Flats is a flower-painted meadow along the Pecos River that acts as the Grand Central Station for trails coming to and from numerous areas of the wilderness. Pecos Falls, 9.5 miles in, is a 50-foot waterfall located in one the most remote and least visited zones. It is possible to follow a loop off Hamilton Mesa and down into the wild and scenic Pecos River valley to reach both of these natural beauties. Refer to the Pecos Falls USGS map.

14

Hermit Peak

Type: Day hike

Season: June to November

Total distance: 9.2 miles

Rating: Moderate

Elevation gain: 2,700 feet

Location: Pecos Wilderness, 18 miles west-northwest of Las Vegas

Maps: USGS El Porvenir

Getting There

From Las Vegas, take Grand Avenue north, which is also NM 65. At 0.8 mile, you reach a controlled intersection with Railroad Road; turn left toward New World College, which is signed. At 1.1 miles, you reach another stoplight. Turn right onto Hot Springs Road, the continuation of NM 65. Shortly past the turn, you will see a sign for El Porvenir. Use this as a landmark to make sure you're on the right path, as the trailhead for Hermit Peak is in the same direction. At 12.1 miles, after winding through the river canyon and entering a valley of horse pasture and farmland, you pass through the town of Gallinas. Straight ahead is Hermit Peak, the rounded massif whose middle section stretches to more of a point. At 12.5 miles, the road forks. Bear right onto FS 261, which leads to El Porvenir Campground. Another 2.7 miles down (15.2 miles total), you reach a small parking area and the trailhead for Hermit Peak Trail 223.

The Trail

Written about in an essay by Rick Bass and taken as the title of a novel by Michael McGarrity, Hermit Peak comes by its name thanks to an Italian recluse by the name of John Augustiani who lived on the mountain to stay out of the public eye. Today people visit this high, flat perch to take in the sharp contrast between the terminus of the Rocky Mountains protruding from the north and the beginnings of the Great Plains spreading to the eastern horizon.

The hike begins in a ponderosa pine and fir forest along Porvenir Creek. You cross over a road around 0.2 mile in and follow the sign for Hermit Peak Trail 223. The pathway is a bit uneven and rocky and gains elevation moderately. In spring and

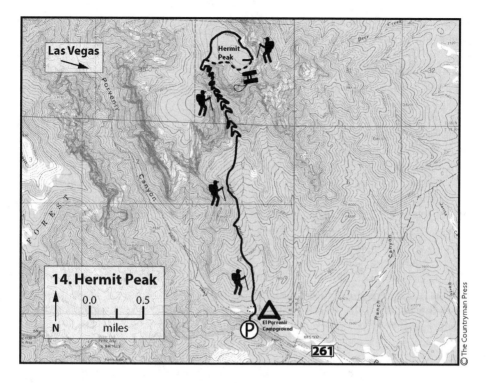

early summer you will find paintbrush, sunflowers, daisies, and buttercups. Much of the rest of the relatively sparse understory consists of shrubs like Gamble oak. The trail parallels a creek drainage for a half mile. At about 0.6 mile you cross the creek; stay to the left, continuing along the drainage. The short shrubs with red berries and spoon-shaped leaves are kinnikinnick. Native peoples used kinnikinnick leaves as a diuretic for urinary tract problems and made a form of tobacco that incorporated the dried leaves.

At 0.8 mile the trail arrives at another road. Head left about 40 yards to a sign for Hermit Peak and the continuation of the trail. As encouragement, there are filtered views of a portion of Hermit Peak—a granite batholith that originally pushed forth some 1.4 billion years ago.

After hiking some 2 miles and gaining about 1,000 feet of elevation through a sun-filled forest, you officially enter the 222,673-acre Pecos Wilderness. Tucked in the southeast corner, the hike to Hermit Peak (10,212 feet) is one of dozens available across New Mexico's second largest wilderness area. By 2.2 miles the trail begins to steepen as you approach what looks like an impassible gap. It soon becomes apparent, however, that you can indeed pass through the gap's two rock outcroppings via a couple of switchbacks. This gap will lead you to a plateau or benched section of the mountain for the final easy walk to the broad point of Hermit Peak's summit. Aspen and a few other deciduous trees and shrubs join the forest mix as you slowly gain on the plateau, passing by a small boulder field at the bottom of a sheer cliff at the 3-mile mark.

At 3.9 miles you reach the plateau.

From here you can look across the south-central region of the Pecos Wilderness to the west or view the beginnings of the southwest edge of the Great Plains, stippled with mesas and extinct volcanoes, along the horizon to the east. A short distance down the trail you reach a junction. A covered spring is set in a small clearing here. Heading straight, the trail makes a slow arc to gain the summit. The more road-like path to the right climbs a bit more steeply but directly to reach the opposite end of the broad summit. It is along the summit that you will discover the Hermits' Cave. This is where Augustiani is reported to have lived during his time here.

Continuing straight away, you pass through a grove of aspen as the trail slowly bends along the western side of Hermit Peak. There are more views across the Pecos and a view over man-made Storrie Lake. You also come across another trail junction at 4.5 miles. The trail that makes a sharp downslope turn to the left leads to Lone Pine Mesa 5 miles away.

The summit (4.6 miles) is a great place to camp. There is a fantastic plateau environment up here with slightly higher views toward the Great Plains, and to the north you can see the southern flow of the Sangre de Cristo Mountains coming out of Colorado.

Montezuma's Revenge

Rejuvenate sore muscles by soaking in the hot spring across from the United World College just outside Las Vegas along the road to the Hermit Peak trailhead. It occupies the grounds and castle-like structure of the old Montezuma Hotel. Just off the roadway and punched into what feels like a city sidewalk, pools of marvelously silky, mineral-rich springwater attract locals and tourists alike. The water temperature is ideal for a visit in late fall, winter, and early spring. By the time summer arrives, though, the pools are often unbearably hot.

On the trail to Hermit Peak

Hermit Peak

15

San Pedro Parks Loop

Type: Overnight or multiday

Season: June to October

Total distance: 17.7 miles

Rating: Moderate

Elevation gain: 1,000 feet

Location: San Pedro Parks Wilderness, 8 miles northeast of Cuba

Maps: USGS Nacimiento

Getting There

From Cuba, take NM 126 east, which is signed for the San Pedro Parks Wilderness. At 10.2 miles, turn left at a sign for San Pedro Parks Wilderness and San Gregorio Lake. The road surface changes from pavement to packed dirt. At 12.5 miles, make sure to stay straight, continuing along FS 70 instead of turning left. You reach the trailhead and parking area at 12.8 miles.

The Trail

The San Pedro is known for its natural park zones, lush boggy corridors of grassy meadow cut by slow-moving creeks dotted with whitish granite boulders. Wildflowers splash color on the green canvas in the summer months. Elk abound here, enjoying the bountiful food and ease of movement across this 41,132-acre wilderness. Hiking trails branch out in every direction, shadowing the numerous creeks—20 in all—that etch the parklands. What isn't readily apparent, though, is that this is actually a mountain range. The San Pedro Mountains sit like a flat block above the greater arroyo-fed Rio Puerco valley to the southwest, and they are a continuation of the Sierra Nacimiento uplift to the south and neighbor to the Jemez Mountains. You are in essence working across mountaintops, but without the effort normally required to do so.

This hike is a garden stroll, beginning as a wide, smooth, crushed-rock path through an open forest of fir and aspen with wildflowers like lupine, aster, daisy, and a large patch of false hellebore. During the moist times of spring and after summer rains, you will also spot a great variety of mushrooms. Granite boulders—compliments of the uplift of Precambrian

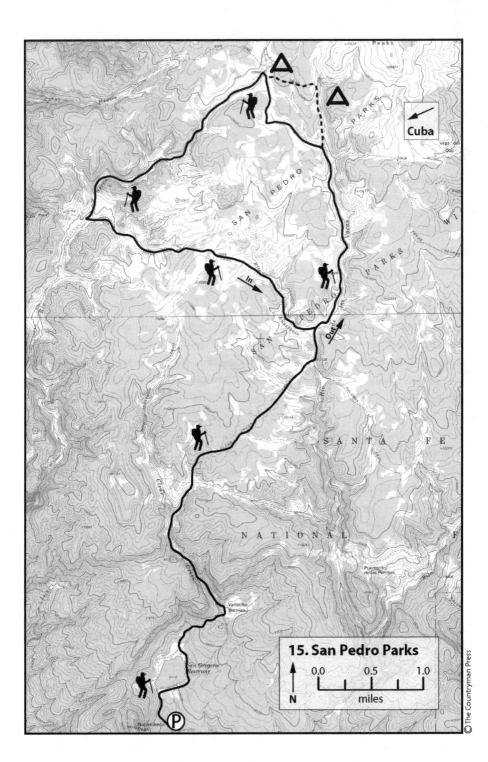

Cuba

15. San Pedro Parks

0.0   0.5   1.0

N   miles

© The Countryman Press

granite hundreds of millions of years ago—are positioned in the forest as if hand placed by landscape artists. Popping up here and there are wild raspberry bushes, with berries ripening around the middle to end of August.

By 0.75 mile you reach man-made San Gregorio Reservoir, set in an open grassy zone colored here and there by the yellow of sneeze weed and the bluish-purple of harebell. Follow the trail to the right, edging around the upper east shoreline. You reenter the forest past the lake and continue the easy-going path you've been on since the trailhead, crossing over sections of elevated walkway where the ground is boggy.

At 1.7 miles you reach a creek crossing beyond a pleasant zone of wildflowers and aspen groves, the trail alternating between a wider path and a narrow hiker's trail. This is the junction for the Vacas Trail to San Pedro Park, which heads left. The trail makes a beautiful run along Clear Creek for 1.3 miles (3 miles total). You will see a path cutting back hard to the left and crossing the creek. Do not take this trail; instead, continue straight just a bit farther along Clear Creek.

About 0.2 mile up you enter the first of many parkland environments on this hike. The trail edges along a grassy, rocky mound, and slightly downslope a feeder creek knifes through the wildflower-lined corridor. By 3.7 miles you reenter the trees and gain a little elevation before starting a flat run that alternates between a corridor of fir trees and open grassy zones choked with false hellebore. You end up stepping across another boggy open parkland at 4.8 miles.

The alternating trees and parkland continue, along with a crossing of the Rio de las Vacas. A trail junction (5.2 miles) lies just a few strides past the other side of the creek. Head left on the Vacas Trail toward San Pedro Parks. In a little over 0.3 mile you reach yet another junction. Continue to the right, still on the Vacas Trail.

This marks the beginning of a beautiful grassy corridor run along the lazy and slightly curvy Rio de las Vacas. The creeks throughout San Pedro are home to native trout. The boggy and wildflower-flecked pocket parklands up to this point already have revealed the uniqueness of the wilderness, but the next phase of the hike definitely places San Pedro in a category all its own. All of these corridors, parklands, and *vegas* (Spanish for "meadows") remain treeless due in part to grazing animals—cattle grazing is still allowed throughout wilderness areas in New Mexico—but primarily because the overly moist ground is not conducive for tree growth.

After nearly a 2-mile run (7.2 miles total) along the Vacas Trail you reach a junction where the Penas Negras Trail goes right and the San Jose Trail to San Pedro Parks goes left. Heading straight will move you into the trees toward an old cabin site. It is approximately 0.7 mile to the cabin, and continuing on this unmaintained trail you can reconnect to the San Jose Trail at San Pedro Parks. Shortly before reaching the 0.7-mile mark, at a point where the trail makes a hard bend to the left away from the creek, there is a hunter's camp down along the creek bank that would make a good overnight spot.

To continue on the hike, take the San Jose Trail through another corridor environment to the wide-open zone a number of square miles in size that is San Pedro Parks (7.8 miles). This whole hike is prime elk country. Also, throughout the boggy zones, including in San Pedro Parks, you may notice a beautiful bluish-purple flower

Parkland on the way to San Pedro Parks

50 Hikes in Northern New Mexico

with a single bloom perched on a stem growing in patches among the grasses— this is fringed gentian. The Rio Puerco is nearby for a water source and there are campsites in the trees.

A couple of round posts mark the way across the boggy section beyond the park. It is difficult, as with other boggy sections along this hike, not to get your shoes wet. By 8 miles you reach the junction with the Los Pinos Trail, which follows the Rio Puerco down a gorgeous tight valley much different from the flat, broad corridor of the Rio de la Vacas. There is a great mix of more heavily treed, steeper-sided slopes with wildflowers, boulders, and broad gentle areas of boggy grasses. It is easy going because of the slight loss of elevation along the way. You have plenty of options for pitching a tent through here. By 9.5 miles, you cross over a creek and are on the edge of another open grassy expanse. But the trail stays in the trees to arrive at the junction with the Anastacio Trail at 9.8 miles. Head left (east) here.

You pass through another boggy section along here. Roughly a half mile along (10.3 miles total) you pass into a narrow corridor. Trails run along the left and right sides, but you should stay to the right, following the round posts. By 11 miles you reach a point where the corridor forks, with options to the right and straight ahead. Two or three round posts mark this spot and forest service blazes—a small round mark where the bark has been removed above a longer mark—on the trees indicate that you should head to the right. You will also notice the wide pathway leading into the trees.

By 12.2 miles you reach the junction with the Vacas Trail. Head to the right and retrace the 5.5 miles back to the trailhead (17.7 miles total). This hike is surely to become a favorite, whether you visit in the spring, summer, or fall.

Coyotes, Bears, and Cows, Oh My!

A less traveled portion of San Pedro Parks is reached off NM 96 near the town of Coyote. Take FS 103 and FS 93 to the Resumidero Campground. From the campground, you can make a loop of 12 miles or so through parklands like Vega Redondo (Round Meadow) and near Vega del Oso (Bear Meadow) on the way to San Pedro Parks. This hike utilizes a combination of different trails—including the *Vaca* Trail (*vaca* means "cow" in Spanish)—some of which fade out in the meadow areas, so a compass and topographic map are a must. The topographic map you would need is Arroyo Delagua.

16

Ojitos Trail

Type: Day hike or overnight

Season: June to October

Total distance: 10.6 miles

Rating: Moderate

Elevation gain: 1,000 feet

Location: Chama River Wilderness,
23 miles northwest of Abiquiu

Maps: USGS Navajo Peak and
Laguna Peak

Getting There

From Abiquiu, take US 84 north toward
Chama. You pass by the turn for Ghost
Ranch and the visitor center before reaching the signed left turn for FS 151 at 14
miles. Take this dirt road for 9.4 miles,
passing by the Big Eddy boat ramp, to
reach a steel bridge that spans the
Chama River. There is a turnout for parking at 23.4 miles.

The Trail

Known by boaters for its wild and scenic
stretch of whitewater from below the El
Vado Reservoir to Big Eddy, the Chama
River Wilderness is much more than a
strikingly beautiful canyon to view from a
raft or kayak. Tall red, yellow, and brown
mesas frosted by the green of ponderosa
pines are separated by canyon bottoms
that punch in at various points along the
18-mile river wilderness. Yucca and juniper and the delicate blooms of globe-
mallow and tiny white daisies decorate the
landscape. There is only one trail in the
50,300-acre wilderness area, which
leaves an awful lot to be discovered by
cross-country travel. The trail described
here is a worthy experience by itself or as
a springboard into the vast open country
of the wilderness.

From the turnout along the road, cross
over the bridge that spans the Chama
River. You are in a beautiful, broad sagebrush valley edged by colored rock walls
and jutting mesas that resemble fantastical birthday cakes. Approximately 0.2 mile
along the road over the bridge you reach a
ROAD CLOSED sign and a trail marker that
points you straight ahead. At 0.5 mile you
pass through a fence opening and by the
official sign for the Chama River Wilderness. The trail continues to edge along the

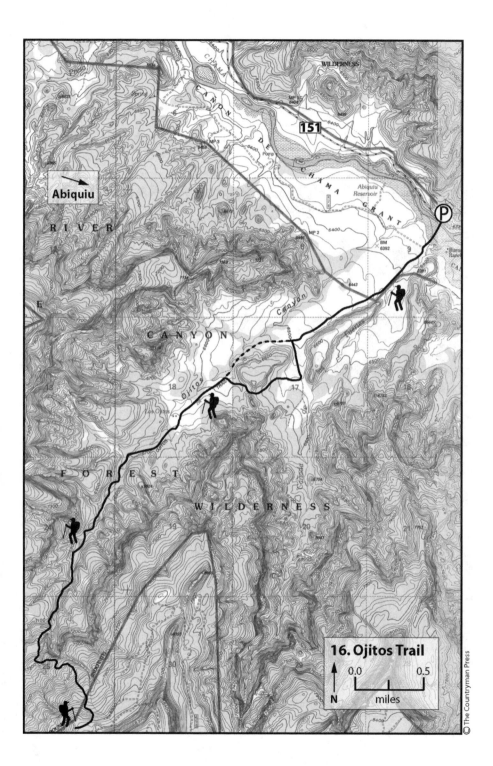

Chama River canyon

pastureland in the direction of a side canyon. The trail markers are round posts with pointed tops.

Chama ("red" from the mispronounced Tewa word *tzama*) surely is the correct name for the boldly colored rock and energetic river that define much of the physical aspect of this place. Another dimension here is the stillness, whether you hike the Ojitos Trail on an early morning in summer or strike out on a crisp autumn weekend. By 1 mile you reach a vague crossroads. The trail heads to the left along a smaller valley floor, through a thick community of sage. A fireworks explosion of small-headed wildflowers appears here after rainy periods. The trail then crosses into pinion pines, a nice treat as this species has suffered greatly throughout New Mexico during the many years of drought.

Through a gap of sorts at 1.5 miles, the trail slings over and into a broader valley/canyon. It is a marvelous area of contrasts: red sandstone, forest-green pinion and juniper, olive-green sage, a rainbow of wildflowers, blue skies often stamped by puffy clouds, and white rocks (gypsum) strewn about like pottery shards. A gate crossing comes at 2 miles, and shortly beyond here you transition into a creekside combination zone of yucca and juniper with Gamble oak and the shade relief of ponderosa pine. The trail crosses from one side of the canyon to the other a number of times during a 2-mile stretch as you continue along a floor bookended by mesas colored in rose, tan, white, and taupe, their tops decorated with juniper and pinion. The life force of the creek also attracts a healthy bird population.

By the 4-mile mark, the trail bends upslope, regaining the canyon floor through a thicker zone of ponderosa pine. You pass by a decent campsite that's not too far from the creek. It is a good option for an overnight, because higher up you will need to pack water. You have growing views of the opposite canyon edge, as well as views across the west-northwest zones of the wilderness. By 5.3 miles you reach a benched zone beneath the short-walled Mesa del Camino. This is a good turn-around point for a day hike or a jump-off point into a cross-country exploration of the wilderness.

Christ Living Off the Grid

At the end of FS 151 you will find the Christ in the Desert Monastery. The sun, captured by solar panels, provides all its electrical needs. There are guest houses for those looking for spiritual retreats and a small church whose tall windows provide a stunning view of the red-rock cliff face. Just before reaching the grounds it is possible to take a short hike into Chavez Canyon. An unimproved trail leads into a slickrock slot canyon, offering a spectacular but easy Utah Canyonlands–type experience. You can find more information at www.christdesert.org.

17

McCauley Warm Springs to Jemez Falls

Type: Day hike

Season: April to November

Total distance: 6.8 miles

Rating: Easy to moderate

Elevation gain: 1,100 feet

Location: Jemez Mountains, 18 miles west of Los Alamos

Maps: USGS Jemez Springs and Redondo Peak

Getting There

From Los Alamos, take NM 501 south for 4.5 miles to the junction with NM 4. Turn right onto NM 4, signed for the town of Jemez Springs. At 23.5 miles, you reach the junction with NM 126. Continue on NM 4 toward Jemez Springs. At 26.5 miles, turn into a large turnout/parking lot near a prominent rock outcropping known as Battleship Rock. There is an official campground and picnic area entrance a short distance down the road, but for a day hike this first lot is where you should park.

The Trail

This outing to McCauley Warm Springs and on to Jemez Falls is a fire and water scenario. The fire originally came in the form of a number of eruptions that took place as recent as 1.1 million years ago, filling the entire Jemez Canyon with volcanic material. Today the fire continues in the geothermal heat that warms the water of McCauley Springs and a number of other springs in the area. A rapid release of water occurred when the natural dam of the Valle Caldera was breached by the push of the San Antonio and East Fork Jemez Rivers surfacing from artesian wells. This water cut the canyon and sculpted the tent rocks you see along the hike, as well as the dazzling water feature of Jemez Falls.

From the parking area you head downhill and through the picnic area to a bridge over the Jemez River. Trail 137 begins beyond a picnic shelter, edging against Battleship Rock and along the lush East Fork Jemez River. It is fairly easy to see how Battleship Rock came by its name. The sharp-edged prow appears to slice through the trees, as if an entire ship will

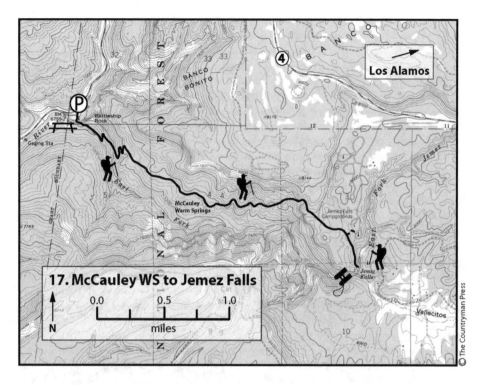

17. McCauley WS to Jemez Falls

0.0   0.5   1.0

N   miles

© The Countryman Press

be cast afloat for a canyon run on the Jemez River. The shape was created by a series of volcanic eruptions that deposited layer upon layer of volcanic ash, which under intensely high heat actually became welded together. This impressive rock formation stands more than 200 feet high.

The habitat is lush with locust, oak, wildflowers, and many other plant and shrub varieties feeding from and contributing back to the riparian life zone. Sandstone is the most prevalent rock, having been laid down nearly 300 million years ago when this area, and much of New Mexico, was sea bottom. There are also beautiful, oily black volcanic rocks called obsidian, monuments to the series of eruptions that created the Jemez River canyon and continue to feed the geothermal heat for at least 15 different hot and warm springs in the area.

Popularity has its price, and unfortunately human visitors wanting to blaze their own paths have created unnecessary trail options around the 0.2-mile mark. Follow the trail heading upslope and to the left. You climb for a short distance, gaining elevation over the river yet still within earshot of it. You also end up above Battleship Rock, which is framed nicely against the western wall of the Jemez River canyon.

Gaining elevation also means entering a different life zone, one more arid and dominated by ponderosa pine, yet decorated with asters and scarlet gilia. By 0.9 mile the trail levels off. It feels like you are walking along a canyon rim, but without any danger, as you move along the northern side of the East Fork Jemez River canyon. A wonderful attribute of this hike to McCauley Warm Springs and then on to Jemez Falls is that in a relatively short dis-

Battleship Rock

tance, with minimal energy output, you can experience a deep backcountry feeling. However, you will have to time your outing for early morning and avoid weekends and holidays to reap this reward.

You arrive at McCauley Warm Springs at 1.5 miles. The water is naturally heated, but the pools are man-made. And the setting is quite nice, with the upper, larger, and more exposed pool feeding the smaller, more shaded pool. Remember, these are considered warm springs so their temperatures range between 85 and 95 degrees. The temperature range in hot springs normally runs from 100 to 115 degrees. Soak your feet or submerse yourself fully for some rejuvenation before the short push on to Jemez Falls.

The springs also provide an oasis for a number of plants and creatures in this particular life zone. Wild roses grow downstream from the bottom pool, creating sustenance for bees during blooming season and food for a variety of bird species in the form of rosehips. And the moss that covers many of the rocks along the warm-water stream is part of the diet for deer in the winter months. It is quite serene to watch the water bend and turn around smoothed boulders and downed trees, dropping in little cascades as it begins its journey to meet the East Fork Jemez River some 700 feet below.

To continue on to Jemez Falls, walk around the top end of the upper pool or follow one of the side trails below the lower pool to reach the main trail. It begins by losing a little elevation and then rises gently on the way to the falls. For most of this hike, the trailbed is level and has a surface of crushed rock. Approximately 0.3 mile past the springs (1.8 miles total), the slope opens up to provide a view across the canyon to some rock outcroppings

that are pushing their way out from between the trees. The coloration of the rock varies from richer reds to brownish-tans to mustard yellow. At 2.5 miles, again across the canyon, another geologic feature displays itself in the form of cone-like conglomerate rock formations with sharp peaks, appropriately called tent rocks. Over time, volcanic eruptions deposited a mixture of ash, pumice, and what is known as tuff (fragmented rock material), then wind and water slowly sculpted the rock into its present form.

Jemez Falls is accessible off NM 4–if you drove to the trailhead from Los Alamos you passed this turnoff. It has a designated campground area that you reach along the trail at 3.1 miles. A few hundred yards downslope, the trail makes a dip and then meets up with a wider trail leading to the falls. A sign there indicates the downslope direction and the ¼-mile distance.

The East Fork Jemez River makes a very slow, lazy turn just before it drops in a stair-step. The final drop is the longest, a free fall of about 20 feet. The total height of the falls is 70 feet. About 20 feet down from the top, there is a beautiful side pool positioned like a watery balcony in the shade. The viewing area for the falls is on top of a whitish rock outcropping. Adding to the pleasantness of the area are views of Los Griegos (10,117 feet) to the west and the nearby ridgeline, which is covered in ponderosa pine and splashed with patches of aspen.

Spend the Afternoon in Ruins and the Evening Recovering

Continuing on NM 4 into the town of Jemez Springs, you pass the Jemez State Monument. It is a mixed site, with ruins of a 500-year-old pueblo known as Giusewa ("Place at the Boiling Waters") to the

Jemez people and a 17th century Spanish mission. The town of Jemez Springs is populated with restaurants, specialty shops, motels, and bed & breakfast operations, all set in a gorgeous, tall red-rock canyon. The town also lives up to its name, offering public-accessible hot springs at Giggling Springs (505-829-9175) and Jemez Springs Bath House (505-829-3303).

18

Box Canyon

Type: Day hike

Season: Year-round

Total distance: 3.8 miles

Rating: Moderate

Elevation gain: 100 feet

Location: Ghost Ranch, 8 miles northwest of Abiquiu

Maps: USGS Ghost Ranch

Getting There

From Abiquiu, drive 11.5 miles north on US 84 to the entrance for the Ghost Ranch Conference Center (the official visitor center is another 2 miles down on the right). The road surface changes from pavement to gravel as you drive into the Ghost Ranch. Approximately 1 mile up, you reach a sign indicating the headquarters to your left and the dining hall to your right. Stay to the right. After paralleling a large open field, in about 0.5 mile you pass through a parking lot behind the dining hall. A very short distance from here you come to a set of posts with various signs; follow the one to the right for Kitchen Mesa (Hike 19). Drive another 0.4 mile (39.9 miles total) to reach the trailhead parking area. Next to where the road is blocked off by a metal cable, you will see

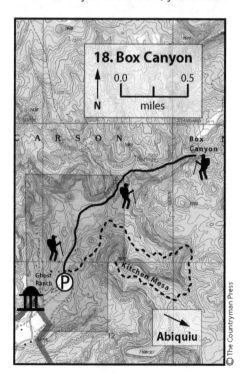

The entrance for Box Canyon

signs for Kitchen Mesa and Box Canyon. Park here for both hikes.

The Trail

Vivid sandstone walls painted in bands the color of red chili powder, white gypsum, and tanned leather stand as blocky book-ends at the beginning of an easy and short-but-adventurous journey along the spring-fed Arroyo del Yeso. The canyon narrows the farther up you travel, eventually reaching the walled-in hollow that gives this place the name Box Canyon.

Starting in the same location as the hike to the top of Kitchen Mesa, the trail forks to the left at the point where the Kitchen Mesa Trail crosses the arroyo. You pass by four or five small rounded adobe huts known as hogans (Navajo style

homes). There are great views of Kitchen Mesa, Chimney Rock to the west, and the mouth of Box Canyon straight away along this portion of the hike. The sandy, road-like path moves through juniper and pinion pine and a prolific collection of saltbush or chamisa, which produces a soft yellow bloom that turns the shrub into an over-sized pom-pom in late summer, lighting up the plateau in a colorful play off the red-rock walls. For those interested in high desert plant life, there are plenty of species to identify, from cholla to prickly pear cactus to greasewood.

By 0.3 mile you reach the junction for Camposanto. This memorial is set against the near cliff wall. It was built as a way for people to honor those who have departed in this place of wild beauty that is Ghost

Ranch. Continuing on the Box Canyon Trail, you step into the creek bed at about 0.5 mile. As you make your way up the narrowing canyon the trail stays along, or actually in, the creek. Before moving on, look up at the near cliff to see a rock feature that resembles an incomplete sculpture of a human.

You cross under an old water pipe and around a bend in the creek before entering a small forest of sorts. You will see a series of eight coffee cans painted black and numbered through here. The first comes at the start of the pseudo-forest run. Pinion pine, juniper, and tall Gamble oak surround you before the trail slips back into the creek environment. This area also is known as Yeso Canyon (*yeso* means "gypsum" in Spanish). The route has been well-traveled and is marked at key places, so just relax and enjoy the experience. Water is present year-round. Sandals with or without neoprene socks wouldn't be a bad idea, although normal hiking footwear is perfectly fine. Be aware that during heavy rains the canyon is not passable, and it is downright dangerous during a flash flood.

Cottonwood trees also dot the canyon. They turn a rich yellow in the fall and, along with the red to rust-brown Gamble oak leaves, make for a welcoming scene. The Upper Camp Trail junction comes at about 1 mile, along with the fifth coffee can marker. The canyon becomes more rugged past here, and you're forced to do a lot of hopping back and forth from one side of the creek to the other. The canyon walls also grow taller, creating the feel of a more remote canyoneering experience. A sign points upward to an eagle's nest perched high on the cliff wall just past the junction. Nests can measure 8 feet in diameter and weigh as much as 1,000 pounds. This one is most likely to be occupied in spring.

The canyon splits at about 1.5 miles. A couple of small, tranquil pools are set on top of one another and big blocks of rock begin to choke the flow of the creek at this point. The eighth marker is located here. It is possible to explore up either canyon; continue straight for access to the terminus of Yeso Canyon.

Paintbrush Renegade

She was born in Wisconsin in 1887 and spent years working on her art in cities like Chicago and New York, but it wasn't until 1929 that the name Georgia O'Keeffe would become synonymous with northern New Mexico. Her sensual interpretation of the surrounding landscape through color and perspective put her work in an unofficial category called "almost abstract." The world was taken by her talents and unique style and paintings of hers like "Pedernal" and "Black Iris" were regarded with the same prestige as works by Picasso and Matisse. Extremely independent—not easy for a woman in her time—O'Keeffe eventually moved to this area, which was even more remote and cut off from the rest of the country than it is today. After the death of her husband, Arthur Steiglitz, in 1946, she continued to live in the area of Ghost Ranch until her death in 1986 at the age of 98.

19

Kitchen Mesa

Type: Day hike

Season: Year-round

Total distance: 3.8 miles

Rating: Moderate

Elevation gain: 550 feet

Location: Ghost Ranch, 8 miles northwest of Abiquiu

Maps: USGS Ghost Ranch

Getting There

From Abiquiu, drive 11.5 miles north on US 84 to the entrance for the Ghost Ranch Conference Center (the official visitor center is another 2 miles down on the right). The road surface changes from pavement to gravel as you drive into the Ghost Ranch. Approximately 1 mile up, you reach a sign indicating the headquarters to your left and the dining hall to your right. Stay to the right. After paralleling a large open field, in about 0.5 mile you pass through a parking lot behind the dining hall. A very short distance from here, you come to a set of posts with various signs; follow the one to the right for Kitchen Mesa. Drive another 0.4 mile (39.9 miles total) to reach the trailhead parking area. Next to where the road is blocked off by a metal cable, you will see signs for Kitchen Mesa and Box Canyon (Hike 18). Park here for both hikes.

The Trail

Ghost Ranch carries a fantastical history that flows from the birth of the great age of dinosaurs to a revolution in American painting to an Indiana Jones–style discovery of natural artifacts that put this fiercely unforgiving place on the world map. The stories are infused with wonderful names like Coelophysis, Chinle sand lands, Dr. Friedrich von Huene, Piedra Lumbre, Chama River, Georgia O'Keeffe, and, of course, the ominously named Ghost Ranch itself, whose symbol, the sun-bleached cow skull and horns, appeared in paintings by O'Keeffe. The journey to Kitchen Mesa is a journey across 200 million years.

On the other side of the cable are the access trails for Kitchen Mesa and Box Canyon. Both are short hikes, and even at a leisurely pace you can easily manage to

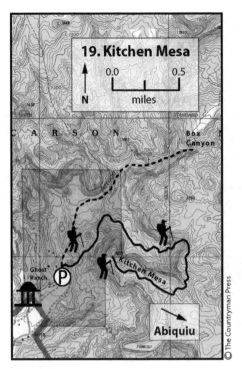

in a zone that sees just 9 inches of precipitation a year.

To the south is the incredibly prominent steep-sloped neck and flat top of Pedernal ("flint" in Spanish). Georgia O'Keeffe memorialized this mountain in numerous paintings, and in a way created the iconic symbol for the high desert of northern New Mexico. This trail has a unique marking system that mainly utilizes large coffee cans painted green with one vertical white stripe. You will see them on the ground, hanging off tree limbs, and capping posts. They are handy for the approach up to and across the first section of the mesa.

At 0.4 mile, the trail makes a steep push up a hill of red sand and down the other side. This is one of the places where excavations took place from the late 1940s into the 1950s, uncovering completely intact Coelophysis dinosaurs. This particular species isn't the missing link between the Triassic and Jurassic periods, but it is an extremely crucial one in determining the progression of the greater species.

The carnivorous Coelophysis was not very big, about the size of a small adult human. Thousands of complete skeletons were found, concentrated in layers near the point where the Kitchen Mesa Trail passes over, and 10 times that amount may still lie buried in the area. The process of preservation through fossilization is well-understood: Silts and soils carried by water buried the dinosaurs shortly after their demise, suggesting that flooding occurred. What can only be speculated about is how so many young and old Coelophysis died at the same time. The most likely theory comes from a more modern comparison with thousands of crocodiles that died along the Amazon after being attracted to a bountiful food source

see the geographic treats that define each in a single day. Start the Kitchen Mesa hike by crossing over the arroyo. The trail makes a tiny push uphill into an open zone of cactus, sage, chamisa, cholla, and yucca, with a bottom-up view of the layered, multicolored birthday cake that is Kitchen Mesa's southwest side.

The various blooming stages of wildflowers, cactus, cholla, and chamisa offer a dramatic contrast to the red-rock environment. A series of wildflowers bloom from spring into fall. Green pitaya cactus—barrel-shaped and usually growing in clusters—produces a scarlet bloom in May. Cholla (pronounced *choi-a*) has a delicate fuchsia-colored bloom in late summer. The chamisa or saltbush, with eight varieties in New Mexico, paints the ground in soft yellow puff balls. These plants and others are reminders of the vitality and diversity of life

Kitchen Mesa

that disappeared because of drought. Perhaps a similar event occurred with the Coelophysis.

Once on the other side of the red hill, you are at the mouth of a small, dead-end valley bottom. The trail continues through a similar mix of plant life, passing by large, smooth sandstone boulders, across a couple of small arroyos, and under the beginnings of a deeper conchoidal arch—sandstone seemingly scooped out with a large spoon from the vertical wall on the northwest side of Kitchen Mesa. It doesn't appear that there is access to the mesa top, but by 0.8 mile you begin a steeper push up a loose rock trail. You will have to do some high-stepping over bigger rocks and eventually a small amount of scrambling. At 1.1 miles, guided by the green

coffee cans, you are below a slot in the wall that requires some effort to make the short ascent to the top. This little climb may not be feasible for small children, older people, or those in poor physical condition.

Once atop the mesa, the trail stays close to the edge and then makes a short push to an upper shelf via a minor scramble. In the last section, before you step on a defined crushed rock trail, the path moves across a staircase-like collection of shale, hundreds of thin layers built up over thousands of years during the Mesozoic era about 150 million years ago.

Another feature here, and really throughout the high plateau desert, is the presence of a very large collection of organisms called cryptobiotic soil. It is clearly visible in the soot black, fist-sized bumps or lumps on the ground. This is a living organism made up in large part by cyanobacteria, but it may also include soil lichens, mosses, green algae, micro-fungi, and bacteria. This crust plays an important role in the ecosystems in which it occurs, stabilizing the soil against the erosive nature of wind and water, absorbing water to the benefit of neighboring plants, and enriching the soil with nitrogen to create a livable environment for other plants. It has an armorlike appearance, but don't be fooled: Cryptobiotic soil is highly susceptible to damage by foot traffic. Depending on the conditions it could take up to 100 years for a section of ground to recover. So stay the course, and stay on the trail that leads across the mesa to a white rock field.

It is a brilliant, easy promenade of 0.7 mile (1.9 miles) to the trail's conclusion, 450 feet above the valley below. From the mesa top (7,077 feet) you can see Pedernal, Abiquiu Lake, Box Canyon, Chimney Rock, the mountains of the Chama River Wilderness, and the Sangre de Cristos to the east. The cream cheese spread of white rock covering Kitchen Mesa from edge to edge is gypsum—made up of sulfate minerals left behind by evaporated sea water.

Just as you should anywhere above tree line or out in the open, you must keep an eye out here for approaching thunderstorms in the summer months. In a matter of minutes, storm cells can build and seemingly collide with each other to create an explosion of lightning and torrential rain. Lightning strikes come in rapid succession and with surprising consistency, repeatedly hitting the ground in the same general area. And rain can fill a typical dry arroyo with 2 to 3 feet of water in 10 minutes. Don't try to outrun it either.

A Bone to Pick

Besides the intact skeleton of a Coelophysis, the Ruth Hall Museum of Paleontology on the grounds of Ghost Ranch also offers fossils of the Rutiodon. A Photostat, the Rutiodon is a parallel ancestor of the crocodile that reached lengths of 16 feet. It was a menacing predator. The Coelophysis and Rutiodon existed some 200 million years ago during the Triassic period. For museum hours and other information about Ghost Ranch, visit www.ghost ranch.org.

20

Cerro Pedernal

Type: Day hike

Season: May to October

Total distance: 7 miles

Rating: Moderate to strenuous

Elevation gain: 1,900 feet

Location: Santa Fe National Forest,
8 miles west-southwest of Abiquiu

Maps: USGS Youngsville and Cañones

Getting There

From the town of Abiquiu, take US 84 for
7.2 miles west to the junction with NM 96,
which is signed for Gallina, Coyote, and
Abiquiu Lake. Turn left and follow NM 96
for 11.2 miles and then make a left turn
onto FS 100. The gravel road climbs to
reach FS 160 in 5.5 miles (23.9 total). Pull
onto FS 160 and park in the open area on
either side of the road.

The Trail

Made into a symbol of the harsh beauty of
the Chama River valley by painter Georgia O'Keeffe, Cerro Pedernal reveals its
true shape on this hike. Viewed from the
north in the Ghost Ranch area, the steep-
shouldered, flat-topped basalt volcanic
structure appears to be a long butte. Its
secret is exposed during the approach,
and even more so from the summit: Pedernal is really a narrow rock band formation, as dramatic as a Hollywood movie
set. Unlike the big screen, however,
Cerro Pedernal offers a visceral experience in the grassland approach, rock
climb–like ascent, and tremendous views
over a vast spread of the Chama River
environment.

Although it doesn't happen often, it
should be noted that the road is actually
accessible to four-wheel-drive vehicles all
the way to the base of the final hike,
scramble, and climb to the top. Regardless, it's a nice hike all the way. You will
enjoy shape-shifting takes of the mountain,
crossing through a band of multicolored
flint, and pausing in a meadow overlook of
the Chama River valley. Pinion pine, ponderosa pine, juniper, Gamble oak, sagebrush, the late-summer-blooming chamisa
(saltbush), and wildflowers blanket the first
0.6-mile stretch. The road bends west

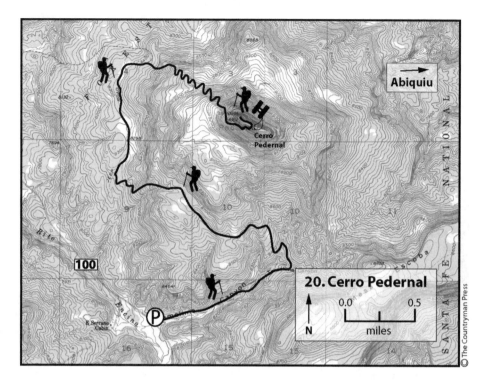

from its northeasterly course, climbing in view of the south face of Pedernal around the 1-mile mark.

The views grow as you climb, including ones over the Rito Encino valley and the Rio Cañones canyon located to the south. By 1.9 miles, the road meets a T-intersection of sorts. Follow the rocky road coming in sharply from the right, not the one bending to the left. After a steep ascent of 0.5 mile (2.4 miles total), you reach the first of a chain of meadows, with Pedernal looming larger and larger over you.

Keep an eye out for rock cairns placed along the road around 2.8 miles, close to the road's end. Following the cairns, you pass through some open space before setting foot on a good trail again. If you miss the start of the trail, you'll need to aim for the sharp western face of the mountain. Stay slightly to the right of center and

you will hit the steep corkscrew trail that leads to a small boulder field at 3.3 miles. Scarlet gilia, wallflower, and lupine light up the grassy meadows.

Cairns guide you to the top of the boulder field and onto a trail that hugs the bottom end of the upper cliff bands around to the south side. In less than 0.2 mile, you pass under a leaning juniper tree. Shortly after, as you scan the wall, you will see a location that reveals the most sensible access to the top. This spot should be marked by a white arrow. If you reach the cave you observed on the hike up, you have gone too far. Just backtrack slowly and you will see this spot. There also may be a small platform of rocks that previous hikers have set up to begin the short climb.

To access the summit of Pedernal you have to climb. The tough section is less than 12 feet high and in climbing vernacu-

Cerro Pedernal's distinctive shape is visible in the distance.

lar would be rated only about a 5.6 in difficulty. Use your own judgment about whether to try it. Once you are above this section, a rough trail moves along to the right. Another scramble/climb is necessary shortly before you reach a chute of sorts on your left. The surface is loose rock, so be careful as you clamber up, especially if there are others behind you.

As you go higher, you pass through some trees and into a small clearing on the top of Pedernal. The mountaintop is about 0.2 mile long and the true summit is on the western end. The vistas do not disappoint from any location up here, with a grand take on the Chama River valley, the Rio Puerco valley, the Jemez Mountains to the south, more distant mountain ranges like the Sangre de Cristos to the northeast, and others to the northwest.

The Mountain God Gave Me

Georgia O'Keeffe said that God should allow her to claim Cerro Pedernal as her own because of her numerous paintings of the landmark. Over her long, vibrant career she managed to create 20 different paintings of the mountain, many of which can be seen at the Georgia O'Keeffe Museum in Santa Fe (www.okeeffemuseum.org). The museum collection has other famous paintings of O'Keeffe's—1,148 paintings and drawings in total—like "Black Lines" and "Pelvis Series Red and Yellow."

21

Lower Cañones Canyon

Type: Day hike

Season: May to October

Total distance: 7 miles

Rating: Moderate to strenuous

Elevation gain: 300 feet

Location: Santa Fe National Forest, 8 miles west-southwest of Abiquiu

Maps: USGS Cerro Del Grant and Polvadera Peak

Getting There

From the town of Abiquiu, take US 84 for 7.2 miles west to the junction with NM 96, signed for Gallina, Coyote, and Abiquiu Lake. Turn left and follow NM 96 for 11.2 miles to FS 100. Turn left onto FS 100 and go 7.3 miles to an unsigned junction. FS 100 continues to the right, another road comes in hard from the left, and a third from the right. Take the road from the right, FS 173, which is recommended for high-clearance vehicles and/or four-wheel-drives. The road drops into Cañones Canyon, reaching a junction at 1.3 miles (27 miles total). Turn left and follow a rutted road 0.2 mile to a small parking area. A fence lines part of the parking area and there is a trail sign.

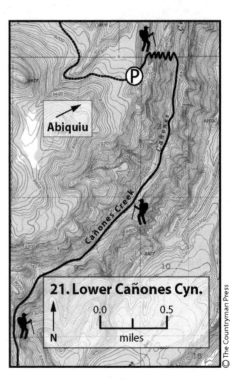

Cañones Creek canyon

The Trail

A rare water source in dry country, Cañones Creek drops from the slopes of the north rim of the Valle Caldera. It runs down a deep canyon whose features range from thick forest to tall sandstone cliff bands to an arroyo in the juniper high desert. This hike is a creek walk of riparian shrubs, plants, and small floodplains decorated in aspen. Cañones Creek Trail is one of 25 trails in New Mexico, and one of more than 900 across the country, that have received National Recreation Trail status.

On the drive in, you will have crossed over Cañones Creek and by the broad canyon mouth yawning into the red-rock country of the Rio Puerco and Chama River valleys. So this trail runs farther up into the green heart of the canyon, with steep forested slopes and cliff bands popping out as you edge along the creek bottom among raspberry and rosebushes and through small pockets of aspen trees. A leisurely stroll along a shaded creek in this region of northern New Mexico is surely a treat for which to be thankful.

A red, white, and light brown cliff band stretches along the opposite side of the canyon from the parking area and is visible for a little while as the trail winds down to the creek in 0.4 mile. Once at the creek, you cross to the other side and work your way through some lush creekside vegetation. By 0.8 mile the trail crosses back over to reach a junction at 1.1 miles. Stay to the left, paralleling the creek.

A meadow follows the junction and the trail dances between the creek side and the trees slightly above. The tree mix is aspen, ponderosa pine, and fir, with an occasional blue spruce. By 1.7 miles, you enter more of an open corridor/floodplain and there is a nice stand of taller aspen on the opposite side of the creek. This is a good spot to turn around, although you could keep going. The total length of the trail is 12.5 miles.

NATIONAL RECREATION

The idea behind the National Trail (NRT) program is to honor ness, but also diversity. Trails with designation include those for hikers, ners, in-line skaters, bikers, horsemen, m torcyclists, snowmobilers, and paddlers. The federal program began in 1968, and as of 2006 there were in excess of 9,000 miles of trails crisscrossing and connecting various regions in every state. Trails like Tent Rocks, Frijoles Canyon, and Winsor are all NRTs, and outings along each are described in this book.

TRAIL
Recreation-
unique-
NRT
...ke

Season: May to October

Total distance: 6 miles

Rating: Moderate

Elevation gain: 1,100 feet

Location: Valle Caldera Reserve,
5 miles west of Los Alamos

Maps: USGS Valle San Antonio,
Valle Toledo, Bland, and Redondo Peak

Getting There

From Los Alamos, take NM 501 south 4.5 miles to the junction with NM 4. Turn right onto NM 4 and head 10.8 miles west to the turn for the Valle Caldera Reserve (there is a sign). The gravel road leads to the staging area in the caldera in 1.3 miles (16.6 miles total). All access into the Valle Caldera currently is by reservation only. The best option for checking the availability of hikes and dates is via the web at www.vallescaldera.gov.

The Trail

Violent volcanic eruptions in the lower 48 states have been few and far between in the last couple hundred years. The Mount St. Helens eruption in May 1980 took the country by surprise. Its display of force leveled hundreds of square miles of forest in a matter of seconds and reduced the mountain's height by 1,300 feet. Here in northern New Mexico, a hulking, towering mountain reaching a height somewhere near 11,000 feet erupted over a million years ago with 100 times the force of that Mount St. Helens eruption, completely rearranging the landscape for hundreds of square miles.

Like a skyscraper imploding, the volcano became a sea of volcanic rock. Some geologists believe you can still see a variety of this feldspar on the north slope of Redondo Peak. Volcanic domes formed inside the caldera, and these were eventually covered with grasses and forest growth. Two artesian wells bubble up inside the caldera, the headwaters of the East Fork Jemez River and the San Antonio River. The valley stays moist enough to keep the encroachment of trees at bay. It is a massive and strikingly beautiful open expanse—14 miles across—that is home to

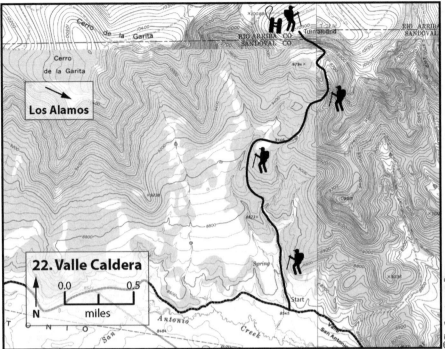

more than 5,000 elk. It also hosts a brilliant bloom of iris in early summer. Hikers are drawn to this unique landscape, which is enjoyed by a variety of creatures.

There are currently three designated hikes in the reserve. The newest is Cerro de los Posos, which provides the highest overlook of the caldera. To hike in the reserve, you must first make a half-hour van ride through the caldera. (Information about reserving a date to hike and where to meet for the shuttle within the preserve is available at www.vallescaldera.gov.) On an early morning hike, you will more than likely spot many elk finishing up the last of their feeding before moving into the trees. It isn't unusual to see 80 to 100 head of elk. The Valle Caldera has been under some form of domesticated grazing for more than 130 years, beginning with huge flocks of sheep tended to by Basque shepherds and continuing today with cattle that still graze sections of the preserve, but in very small numbers.

The Cerro de los Posos hike follows an old logging road to the upper reaches of the north rim of the caldera. The outing is mostly about the tour across the caldera and the sweeping panoramic views. The hike itself is pretty straightforward, as you simply follow a road for 3 miles to a high overlook. For an even grander vista, climb to the open grassy ridgetop. The first 2 miles are set in the trees. At 2.2 miles the road breaks out onto the lower end of the open slope. From here it moves cross-slope, arriving at a gate at around 3 miles. Past the gate, you have access to the grassy slope that leads up to a higher overlook. The road continues on to another gate and the reserve boundary.

You will have approximately five hours

The San Antonio River in the Valle Caldera

to complete this hike and/or explore other areas around this trail. Currently, reserve rules require that you stay on the road because geologists and anthropologists are still assessing the caldera and want uninvestigated areas left undisturbed. The forest around the caldera is a mix of ponderosa pine, fir, spruce, and aspen. The aspen are magnificent in the fall, golden yellow puddles of light set on a canvas of green.

Good Enough to be the Real Thing

Hollywood has been to the Valle Caldera a number of times, with movies like *The Gambler* starring Kenny Rogers and *The Missing* starring Tommy Lee Jones shooting here. Near the entrance to the park sits a homestead that has never been lived in that was used for the movie *Fight Before Christmas*. Another set was created for the movie *The Shootout* starring Gregory Peck, and it was used for other productions too. It was built well enough that the buildings are still used today for housing and storage.

23

Cerro Grande

Type: Day hike

Season: May to October

Total distance: 4 miles

Rating: Moderate

Elevation gain: 1,200 feet

Location: Bandelier National Monument, 5 miles west of Los Alamos

Maps: USGS Bland

Getting There

From Los Alamos, tal
miles to the junction
onto NM 4 and head
total) west to a parkir
just before the left tur.. .u. r⌐ 289.

The Trail

This hike lives up to its name "Grande" with a high eastern rim overlook of the Valle Caldera and views across the heart of canyon-edged Bandelier and the recently fire-deforested peaks of the Dome Wilderness. Sunrises and sunsets are spectacular from this easy-to-access peak.

You pass through a ponderosa pine forest and a loose collection of aspen trees at the beginning of this 2-mile trek. The area only recently was opened to the public, and even though no official trail was con-

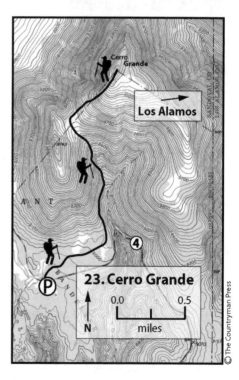

Slope leading to Cerro Grande

structed, the amount of visitation has created a very pleasant approach. The "nontrail" follows a series of yellow diamonds mounted to the trees. The flat, benched zone ends at 0.3 mile and the trail then begins a rollercoaster run to the 1-mile mark. The trail gains the slopeside above young Frijoles Creek, which was one of the life forces to the Pueblo community of Bandelier 10 miles downstream. Across the way, thicker groves of aspen decorate the hillside and bluebell, paintbrush, and scarlet gilia brighten the terrain along the trail. Deer, elk, and coyote also make their home here.

The trail moves away from the drainage, slipping through the trees and gaining elevation. By 1.6 miles, the trail enters the bottom end of the grassy corridor that leads to the summit of Cerro Grande Peak (10,199 feet). The incline is steep through here, as you gain 600 feet in the next 0.4 mile. Your efforts are rewarded by the 2-mile mark, with balcony-style views across a vast amount of the Valle Caldera. The highpoint due west is Redondo Peak, standing 11,254 feet. The Sangre de Cristo Mountains loom large across the Rio Grande. The bulky mass in the distance to the southeast is the Sandia Mountains. A prominent cliff band is visible in the upper end of Frijoles Canyon, as the creek makes a dogleg bend to the left.

Dome Wilderness Fire
The fire began on April 25, 1996, and by the time it was finished, it had burned some 6,000 acres, most of the Dome

Wilderness. The intensity of the fire took down a forest and left behind a charred wasteland—and enumerable treasures. Various scientific groups quickly flocked to the area to begin analysis and exploration. Some specialists were looking at the effects of the sediment runoff that would occur in the streams below the steep slopes now that the holding effect of a living forest was gone. And with the blanket of trees removed, archeologists were able to discover 69 new sites of interest.

24

Bearhead Peak

Type: Day hike

Season: June to October

Total distance: 9.4 miles

Rating: Moderate

Elevation gain: 800 feet

Location: Santa Fe National Forest, 12 miles southwest of Los Alamos

Maps: USGS Redondo Peak, Bland, Canada, and Bear Springs Peak

Getting There

From Los Alamos, take NM 501 south 4.5 miles to the junction with NM 4. Turn right onto NM 4 and head 11.2 miles west to the left turn for FS 280. The dirt/packed-gravel road is not marked along NM 4 coming from Los Alamos. So as soon as you move beyond the edge of the Valle Caldera, watch for a FS 280 sign about 35 feet up on the left. If you pass the sign for the Jemez National Recreation Area on NM 4, you've gone too far. At 2.2 miles along FS 280, you reach a junction: FS 280 continues to the right and the road straight ahead is closed. The rocky road off to the left is FS 282, and this is your turn. This road is accessible only for high-clearance, four-wheel-drive vehicles. At 3.1 miles (21 miles total), you pass by an open area on your right that leads to a large meadow beyond. Park your vehicle in the first open area. The road continues for another 0.4 mile, but there isn't adequate parking farther along.

The Trail

Ridge-running with access to two different peaks, vistas across the rugged back-country terrain of the Jemez Mountains, and a crow's nest–style lookout all await you on this seldom visited hike. Bearhead Ridge rises above the volcanic cliff bands of Peralta Canyon to the west and the former mining community of Bland in Bland Canyon to the east. It curls from south to east to finish on the summit of Bearhead Peak, the site of an old fire lookout.

There are several trail options a short trek from where you parked. The trail to the right slips down into the canyon bottom of Peralta. The trail to the left moves across Woodward Ridge to an overlook of Bland. And straight away the trail leads pleasantly

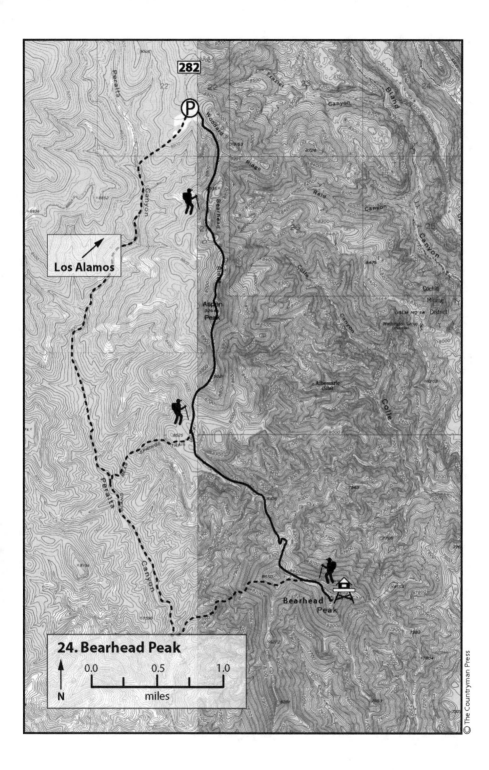

24. Bearhead Peak

Los Alamos

Bearhead Peak

0.0   0.5   1.0

miles

N

282

© The Countryman Press

Bearhead Peak rises in the distance.

across Bearhead Ridge for the first 0.2 mile before it begins popping up and down—but mostly up. There are views of the Sangre de Cristo Mountains, the Dome Wilderness, and Cochiti Reservoir as you move through a mix of ponderosa, fir, and Gamble oak. Wildflowers from aster and bluebells to scarlet gilia and sunflowers grow along the ridge.

At 0.8 mile you come to what looks like a fork in the trail. Stay to the right as you gain more of the northern slope of Aspen Peak (9,244 feet). The trail is rarely maintained, so there may be some downfall with which to contend, but the pathway is relatively easy to follow. Long, round-topped Aspen Peak is reached at 1.5 miles, and by 2 miles you are above an open slope of lichen-spotted volcanic rock

and a healthy population of Gamble oak.

The route from here can be a little tricky. The key is to stay to the right, hugging the edge as a definitive trail does its best to steer clear of the oaks. By 2.3 miles, the trail begins to bend to the southeast, passing through the bottom end of the open slope and nearly down the middle of a stand of aspen. It then curls more to the south before turning southeast again and gaining some elevation to reach an open ridgetop with great views of some columnar volcanic cliff bands in Peralta Canyon at around 3.1 miles. You continue by dipping down to a small saddle before moving cross slope and punching up a steep section to a trail junction at 3.9 miles.

A sign indicates that Bearhead Peak

stands to the left. The trail to the left of Bearhead leads down into Colle Canyon. The one to the right accesses Peralta Canyon. And a relatively easy 0.4-mile jaunt (4.3 miles total) leads you to the small clearing of Bearhead Peak (8,711 feet). Instead of the typical cabin-style structure, lookouts lived in wall tents and climbed a 25-foot tower to reach the crow's nest for a good view of the area. That tower still stands today, barely raising its chin above the ever-growing trees.

You Take the High Road, I'll Take the Low Road

Instead of stepping along Bearhead Ridge, move downslope at the beginning of the hike into Peralta Canyon, following a spring-fed creek before turning upslope to gain the summit of Bearhead Peak. The trail, like many in this area, is unmaintained. Bring a map and compass or GPS and be prepared for some adventure along this alternate route.

25

Dome Wilderness

Type: Day hike

Season: June to November

Total distance: 6 miles

Rating: Moderate

Elevation gain: 1,500 feet

*Location: Dome Wilderness,
10 miles south of Los Alamos*

*Maps: USGS Bland, Frijoles,
Cochiti Dam, Canada*

Getting There

From Los Alamos, take NM 501 south 4.5 miles to the junction with NM 4. Turn right, or west, onto NM 4 and drive just over 6 miles (10.5 miles total) to FS 289, where you turn left (the road is signed). The road surface is gravel. Approximately 2.2 miles up you pass a parking area; continue straight on FS 289 toward the Dome Wilderness. At 7.2 miles (17.7 miles total), there is a sign for the Dome Wilderness and Dome Lookout, along with a list of trails. Turn left here onto FS 142. Because of the poor road condition, four-wheel or all-wheel drives are recommended, but you can continue, up to a point, with a high-clearance, two-wheel-drive vehicle. At 3.5 miles (21.2 miles total), you reach a small parking area just before a closed gate blocks the road to Dome Lookout.

The Trail

On maps, the Dome Wilderness appears as an odd appendage to the 32,727-acre Bandelier Wilderness. And the 5,200-acre Dome Wilderness indeed was created in 1980 as the western extension of the more famous Bandelier. The Dome is its own unique place, however, set in a small sub-range called the San Miguel Mountains, with highpoints like St. Peters Dome (8,464 feet) and Cerro Picacho (8,113 feet). It is found low in Sanchez Canyon, which is 500 feet deep at points. The landscape was once known for its pine-covered slopes and hidden cliff outcroppings, but a fire in 1996 took down 75 percent of the trees. Today it is a stark place of openness and rebirth—still worthy, still its own environment, connected but separate from Bandelier.

Because the Dome ajoins Bandelier National Monument, there are access trails into that park at the beginning and turn-

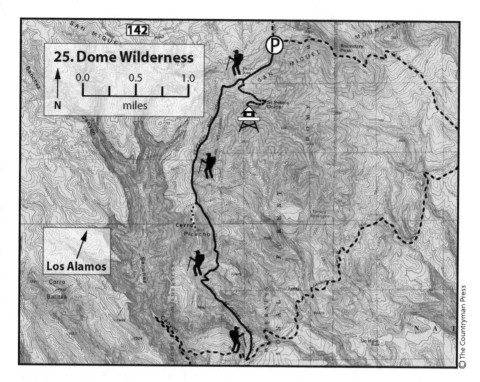

0.0   0.5   1.0

N   miles

Los Alamos

around point of this hike. Boundary Peak Trail 427 and Capulin Trail 116 are accessible at the start. To hike Dome, move past the barricade and follow the road 0.7 mile to the St. Peters Dome Trail, marked by a sky-blue post. This place is in transition, and it is estimated that it will take 150 years for a forest to regrow to pre-fire stature. Regardless, it is a stunning setting with wide views over the leathery folds of the Rio Grande canyon, a series of big basins, striking sharp-toothed Boundary Peak (8,300 feet) in the near distance to the northeast, and other mountainscapes of the Jemez Mountains.

The lookout, visible from here, is accessed by continuing on the road another 0.6 mile. It is no longer regularly staffed, but it still offers a nice view of the surrounding area and you can explore the easy-to-follow ridgeline to the east. The St. Peters Dome

Trail immerses you in the area's new growth. The current plant mix consists of grasses, wildflowers like harebell, sunflowers, and scarlet gilia, and a growing population of Gamble oak. The luscious growth has attracted larger mammals, like deer, elk, and bear, back into this zone.

The trail curves around the west slope of St. Peters Dome and through a rare stand of mature pine trees to reach the upper end of a long saddle at around 0.8 mile. The tall peak to the south is Cerro Picacho. A treeless basin stretches between the two peaks to the east. The scouring effect of the fire has made some of the basalt volcanic rock more prominent, so much so that at points it appears to be still cooling down from a recent eruption. Other wildflower blooms you may see include daisy, aster, nodding onion, and golden rabbit brush. As the area is open and arid, yucca and cactus are also common through here.

The trail fades, but barely, at points as you cross over the spine of the saddle in a southerly direction. Cairns set along here provide further reinforcement that you are on the right path. By 1.2 miles, you pass through a heavier collection of basalt rock before entering the beginnings of a thick cluster of Gamble oak along a midline trail that cuts across Cerro Picacho's east-northeast slope. By 1.6 miles, you enter a stretch of unusual, sometimes castle-like rock formations. Wind and water shaped this rock material, which is called tuff. There also is a broad mesa zone in the near distance that can be explored easily by dipping off-trail a short distance farther along.

At 2 miles, the trail switchbacks into a small canyon decorated with a nice collection of ponderosa pine. It is the only stretch on this hike that offers relief from the sun. By 2.3 miles, you reenter the open space of loose rock and the high Pajarito Plateau plant mix. The stout range you can see to the south-southwest is the Sandia Mountains. By 3 miles you reach a cholla and sunflower zone, along with the junction for Turkey Springs and the hike's turn-around point.

If you head to the left, you could work your way down to a canyon bottom before passing into Bandelier National Monument and on to Turkey Springs (dogs are not allowed in Bandelier). It is possible to pass through the park, which would be 6.5 miles, to make this a loop option for a longer day or an overnight hike. You could also venture up the arroyos into the basin between St. Peters Dome and Cerro Picacho, and back up to the ridge for a cross-country trip back to the trailhead. Of course, just heading back along the trail will make for a rewarding return hike, too.

Sanchez Canyon and the Summit of Cerro Picacho

Cerro Picacho can be summited by following the trail to the right at the junction. It bends back to the north to work up Sanchez Canyon and past a waterfall. Then a steep off-trail ascent takes you to the top. The north slope offers another route up Cerro Picacho. From the saddle you crossed over on the trail from St. Peters Dome, you can scramble up the steep slope for nearly 1,000 vertical feet to the summit. As you can tell, there are plenty of cross-country options from which to choose, especially with the forest cover now gone—at least for the next century or so.

The fire-scarred landscape surrounding the Dome Wilderness lookout

26

Bandelier Canyon Loop

Type: Overnight

Season: May to November

Total distance: 19.1 miles

Rating: Moderate

Elevation gain: 1,500 feet

Location: Bandelier National Monument, 12 miles south of Los Alamos

Maps: USGS Frijoles and Bland

Getting There

From Los Alamos, take NM 501 south 4.5 miles to the junction with NM 4. Turn left onto NM 4 and travel 5.7 miles to the entrance for Bandelier. There is an entry fee of $12 per vehicle, which is good for seven days of access. You can also use your National Parks Pass if you have one. From the entry gate, the road descends into Frijoles Canyon to reach the parking area and visitor center in 3.1 miles.

The Trail

Bandelier National Monument is primarily a wilderness area. Only a small percentage of its 32,727 acres are outside this designation. The Bandelier Canyon Loop Hike takes you away from the bustle of civilization—present and past—of Frijoles Canyon and across open mesas to the rim of breathtaking Alamo Canyon, the doorstep of the once vibrant Yapashi Pueblo, and down through the wild and beautiful Upper Frijoles Canyon. Your sights will be set on the Yapashi Ruins, but there are some real treats along the way.

To begin, cross over the vehicle bridge by the visitor center and walk along the road for less than 0.1 mile to a trail that cuts uphill by some outhouses. Shortly after starting down this trail there is a signed junction. The Yapashi Trail continues uphill, eventually gaining the rim of the southwest wall of Frijoles Canyon. As you climb, views of the northeast wall grow bigger, as does the aerial view of the various ruins from Tyuonyi to Long House to Alcove House farther up canyon. Even though Dr. Edgar Lee Hewett is rightfully credited with being the energy behind the preservation of this area (established in 1916), the national monument takes its name from the Swiss-born archeological

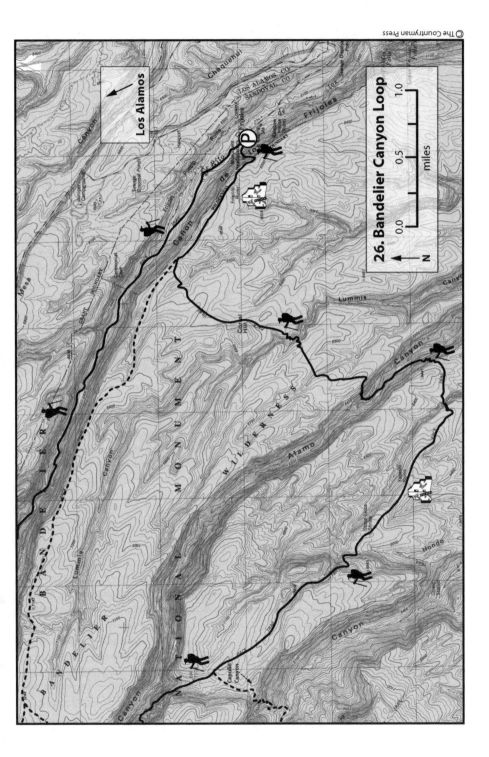

26. Bandelier Canyon Loop

Los Alamos

Yapashi Ruins

pioneer Adolph F. A. Bandelier, whose multiyear exploits of the Southwest included explorations of the ruins of Frijoles Canyon.

At 0.5 mile you reach the canyon rim. From here you have an excellent overview of the surrounding landscape: the forested rise of the Jemez Mountains to the northwest, the Sangre de Cristo Mountains to the northeast, and the stout Sandia Mountains to the east. To the southwest the terrain alternates from rim views to canyon bottoms, with a succession of seven different canyons in a 10-mile stretch. This hike crosses into three of these canyons. This greater geographic area is the edge of the Pajarito Plateau, densely layered by a collection of massive eruptions from what is known today as the Valle Caldera.

The soft ash has been worn and shaped by the run of water over a million years, like a rake dragging tracks in a dirt hill.

The trail edges the rim for another 0.5 mile or so before you reach an unexcavated site called Frijolito. It was occupied in the late 1200s and is estimated to have 70 to 80 rooms. A trail moves south to reach the Rio Grande in approximately 4.5 miles, but you want the trail that continues up canyon to reach a junction for the Yapashi Ruins at 1.3 miles. If you continued straight, you would stay along a beautiful rim trail that eventually drops back into Frijoles Canyon at the Upper Crossing.

The environment is definitely high and dry, with lots of juniper, yucca, cactus, cholla, and, of course, outrageously beautiful bursts of wildflowers in spring and

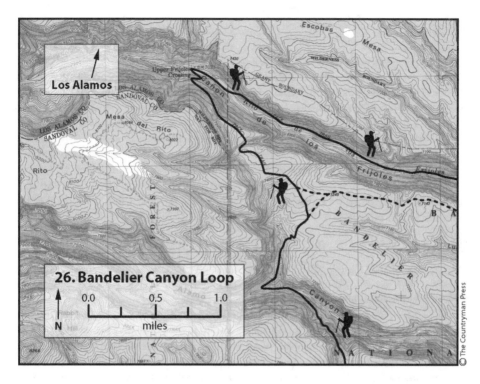

26. Bandelier Canyon Loop

Los Alamos

0.0   0.5   1.0

N   miles

© The Countryman Press

after heavy periods of rain through the summer. As you approach shallow Lummis Canyon, the trees are in greater abundance, including some ponderosa pine in the bottom of the canyon. You make a quick turn and twist to cross into the canyon, stepping over a wet or dry creek bed and gaining open views again by the 2.3-mile mark. The stripped but still majestic highpoints to the east are part of the Dome Wilderness, hit hard by an intense, sweeping, 6,000-acre fire in 1996.

By 2.9 miles the trail noticeably changes to a pumice surface, a remnant of the volcanic blasts from a million years ago. As you round a corner, more than likely admiring the interesting rock formations along the trail, you are hit with a spectacular view of the chasm that is Alamo Canyon. The canyon is only 500 feet deep at this point, but it's broad—¼

mile or so across—with ruggedly stark rock walls. Most of its physical impact comes in the seemingly sudden appearance of the canyon. A steep switchback trail takes you 0.5 mile to the canyon bottom. Again, depending on the winter snowpack, the creek may or may not have water. The trail passes by conical rock formations with boulders balancing on the tips before starting the ascent back out the canyon via the opposite wall. It is a strenuous push, but you reach the rim at the 4.2-mile mark.

By 4.7 miles you have gained much closer views of the Dome Wilderness and arrived at a trail junction. The sign for Yapashi directs you to the right (northwest). In another 0.6 mile you reach the former Yapashi Pueblo. Short rock walls line out what used to be multistory buildings and homes. This community was made up of several hundred people who subsisted by hunting, gathering, and farming. Their most consistent water source was in Capulin Canyon. The most prolific community members today are the cholla, typically sprouting a magenta-colored bloom in summer and after heavy rains.

At 5.7 miles there is a junction for the Dome Lookout and Upper Crossing. Continue toward Upper Crossing in the direction of some large, rounded boulders that mark the entrance to a small side canyon. The trail climbs briefly before entering the ponderosa pine canyon at 6.2 miles. The scenery shifts to a combination grassy zone and pine forest for 0.5 mile. At 7.1 miles you reach the junction with Capulin Canyon. Head toward the canyon to reach a water source and campsite in 1 mile.

Doubling back to continue the loop, you reach the upper section of Alamo Canyon at 7.3 miles. The canyon here is much more treed than it was where you crossed previously, but it still has an impressive, expansive feel. The trail drops to the canyon bottom and a creek crossing at 8.1 miles. A shorter, far less steep ascent takes you back out of the canyon and through a forested section to a more open zone with views across Frijoles Canyon.

There are two junctions close to one another. The first, at 9 miles, is for the rim trail that leads back to the visitor center in 7 miles—this is an option if you want to shorten the hike. The next junction, at 9.2 miles, is a shortcut for hikers coming out of Frijoles Canyon who want to access the rim trail. Stay to the left to reach yet another junction at 9.5 miles, this one marking

Alamo Spring and Ponderosa Campground. Continue toward Upper Crossing and the campground, descending into a lush, creek-fed zone with healthy ponderosa pines and a diverse collection of plant life.

At 11 miles you will have made Upper Crossing. Head to the right, downstream along Frijoles Creek in a fantastic canyon environment, to eventually reach Alcove House and the main canyon ruins and visitor center beyond. There are a number of creek crossings along the first 4 miles or so of this stretch, along with some campsites. The canyon expands and contracts through here, with blocky rock walls in alternating colors of orange, red, gray, and tan. There is a trail the whole way, but the setting creates the feeling that you're exploring a wild, unvisited place.

Alcove House is at 15.9 miles. The easy creekside trail continues for another mile or so back to the visitor center and parking area (17.1 miles).

Stone Lions

A very short distance past the Yapashi Ruins is a sacred site of native peoples. The twin rocks are called the Stone Lions because of their resemblance to reclining lions, which guard the entrance to the dwelling of a supernatural being. It is extremely rare to come across sculptures of this size anywhere among tribes of the Southwest. Even today its spiritual significance is strong enough that Zuni men make journeys of 400 miles here as a rite of passage into manhood.

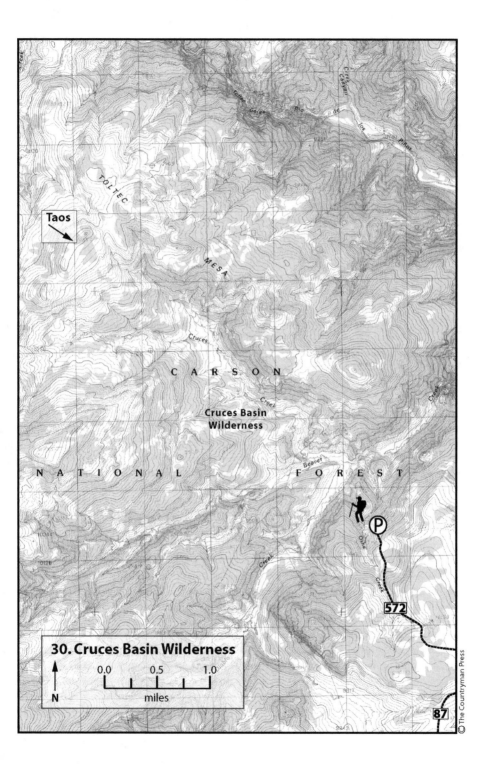

Taos

TOLTEC

MESA

Cruces

CARSON

Cruces Basin
Wilderness

Beaver

NATIONAL   FOREST

Oñas

Creek

572

30. Cruces Basin Wilderness

0.0   0.5   1.0

N   miles

87

© The Countryman Press

Elk are common in the Cruces Basin Wilderness.

Once down in the creek valleys, you have options for gaining the high ground up along Osha Creek or toward the northwest corner of the wilderness onto Toltec Mesa. From the parking area, you can stay high by moving north-northeast on a vast open high-country grass zone that hugs the rim for 2 miles, interrupted by miniature forests of spruce or aspen, before reaching the tight, steep Lobo Creek canyon. This area is teeming with elk and deer, and you may see pronghorn, coyote, and bear. Flowers to identify include daisy, aster, paintbrush, scarlet gilia, fleabane, wild rose, and wild strawberries.

All Aboard!

A significant former lifeline for the mining industry is memorialized today in the wonderful narrow-gauge rail line between Chama, New Mexico, and Antonito, Colorado. Stitching its route along the northern boundary of the Cruces Basin Wilderness, the Cumbres & Toltec Scenic Railroad is a section of the extended rail line that once connected Durango, Colorado, to Denver in the late 1800s. The railway moved minerals like silver and gold that were extracted from the various mining operations along the route. Today the train transports tourists from the middle of June to the middle of October. For more information, visit www.cumbrestoltec.com or call 505-756-2151.

32

Latir Loop

Type: Overnight or Multiday

Season: June to early November

Total distance: 13 miles

Rating: Moderate to strenuous

Elevation gain: 3,400 feet

Location: Latir Wilderness, 25 miles north of Taos

Maps: USGS Latir Peak

Getting There

From Taos, drive north on NM 522. At 0.4 mile, the road, which is signed for Pueblo del Norte, splits; stay to the left. Approximately 4 miles up you reach a stoplight. Continue straight on NM 522 toward Questa. You reach Questa and the junction with NM 38 at 25.4 miles. Turn right at the stoplight onto NM 38, going east toward Red River. In approximately 0.7 mile, turn left onto Kiowa Road, which eventually becomes FS 138. (The turn also is signed for Cabresto Lake.) One mile up, you come to a stop sign at a T-intersection. Turn right, again following the sign for Cabresto Lake. At 2 miles (29.1 miles total), the road surface transitions from pavement to gravel and you arrive at another stop sign. Turn right and continue down FS 138 for 3.4 miles (32.5 total miles) to the sign and left turn for FS 134A to Cabresto Lake. This road is rocky and somewhat steep and narrow. High-clearance, four-wheel-drive vehicles are recommended. In 2.2 miles (34.7 miles total) you reach a good-size parking lot. The trailhead is located here, and there are picnic tables and outhouses.

The Trail

The Latir Loop offers a hidden lake setting reminiscent of regions in Montana, marvels resembling the Scottish Highlands, and a network of alpine ridges connecting gorgeous basins similar to those found in the Colorado Rockies. Under-visited and undervalued, the Latir Wilderness holds backcountry experiences uniquely its own. Although man-made, Cabresto Lake is a beautiful gateway into the wilderness area. Most visitors drive up to the lake to picnic, fish, and take short walks. Very few venture up to Heart Lake, and even fewer continue

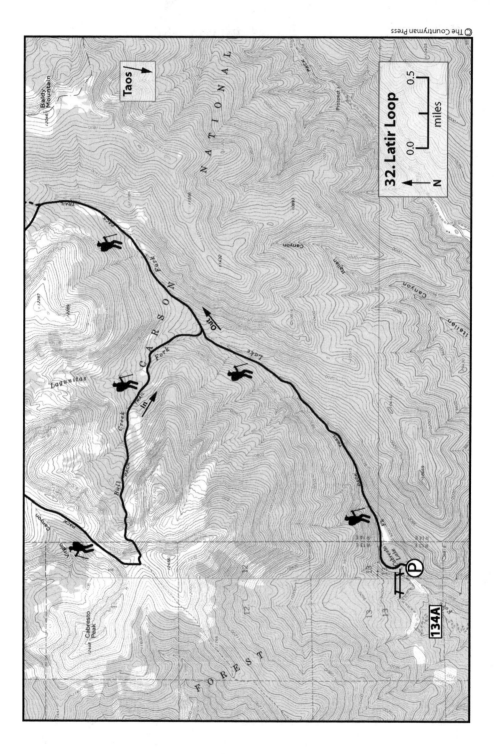

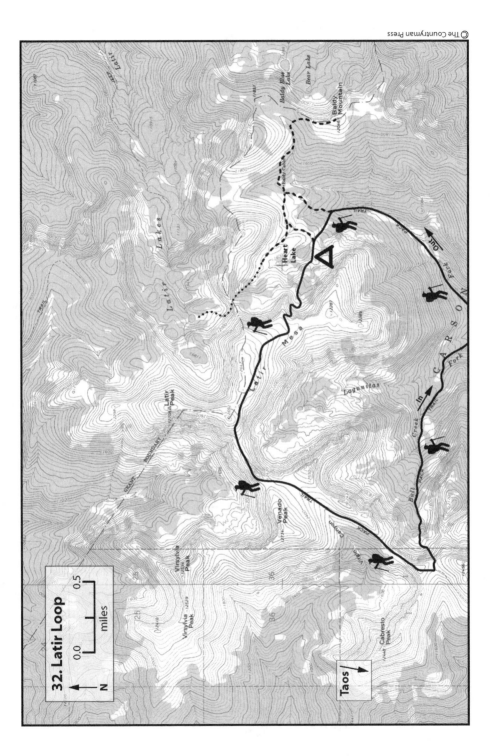

Latir Loop

beyond onto the Latir Mesa and eventually to the incredible alpine settings of pointed peaks and massive basins.

The trail leaves from the parking area and runs above the west shoreline of the lake. A number of spur trails, however, slip steeply down to lake level. It is 0.5 mile to the opposite end of the lake, a lush marshy zone of tall wavy grasses and other aquatic plants fed by Lake Fork Creek. The trail spends nearly all of the next 4.8 miles to Heart Lake edging along Lake Fork, the first portion through a rich riparian environment. There are a number of wildflowers like asters, cow parsnip, and buttercups as you move north up the drainage, immersed in a mixed forest of fir and aspen. At 0.7 mile, the trail reaches the official entrance into the 20,506-acre Latir Wilderness and a small creek crossing.

You may notice a short shrub with a cluster of shiny red berries growing along here; this is baneberry. The leaves, roots, and especially the berries are poisonous. The vegetation is less lush along this stretch, but no less interesting, with bluebells, scarlet gilia, wild strawberry, and wild raspberry bushes growing out from rock sections along the trail. And, as mushroom hunters know, in spring and after periods of heavy rain there are fungal treasures to be found along the forest floor.

At 1.8 miles, the trail enters a slightly more open zone that offers views of the southeast end of Latir Mesa. It is a nice reprieve from the tree cover. On your topographic map, the ridgeline and mountain system of Latir Mesa, Latir Peak, and Cabresto Peak resemble an amoebic subalpine and alpine mass. The Bull Creek Trail junction and the confluence of Bull Creek and Lake Fork come at 2.5 miles. Continue toward Heart Lake, crossing Lake Fork.

The trail starts a steady climb from here, cruising along the creek and taking occasional side trips upslope. At 4.1 miles, you reach the junction with the Baldy Mountain Trail. Baldy Mountain is a 3-mile journey that pushes steeply through the forest before breaking out above tree line. There are great views from the summit of this 12,046-foot peak.

From the junction it is 0.7 mile (4.8 miles total) to Heart Lake. The trail climbs somewhat steeply through the trees and then enters a wide grassy swath, where it parallels the outlet for Heart Lake. This is also the first point along our tour of Latir, where much larger views open up to blocky, grass-topped Latir Mesa beyond the lake, highpoints to the northwest, and Baldy Peak rising above a thick collar of trees. The lake is surrounded by trees and ringed by grasses and wildflowers like cinquefoil. There are campsites on the south end of the lake, and this quiet setting offers a very nice spot to spend the night.

Just before you reach the lake there is a sign to the left for Latir Mesa. After visiting the lake, you will backtrack briefly to this trail to continue the loop hike. The trail passes some large quarry-like piles of rock and takes a steep course through the trees before reaching the bottom end of a basin at 5.2 miles. There is a jumbled archipelago of rock and grass islands the whole way up to the basin rim and the edge of the Latir Mesa. The grassy zones are also home to daisy, paintbrush, and shrubby cinquefoil, providing a nice distraction to the steep, serpentine climb along with a growing overview of Heart Lake and the entire surrounding area. You reach the mesa at 5.6 miles.

The Latir Mesa setting is unique to New Mexico, especially if you arrive when a

Highline junction in the Latir Wilderness

misty fog has settled in. The broad, slightly rounded mesa dead-ends to the southeast, but you can follow the route north and northwest to even more spectacular areas. The mesa is a mix of thick clumpy grasses, large and small rocks, and a variety of hardy-yet-delicate wildflowers.

This is the most difficult section of the hike to follow. The trail is often swallowed up by the grasses, and only by the aid of rock cairns are you able to find the way easily. A good topographic map and compass are a must. It also helps to know that you should stay more toward the crest of the mesa and follow along as it makes a gentle bend to the northwest. It then connects with a short rockslide section that leads to a sharp, narrow saddle between two beautiful basins.

At 6.2 miles you reach a highpoint and then move down to a more discernable trail that crosses a rockslide at 6.6 miles. From the saddle, there are perfect views into the bottom of each basin and to the sharper highpoint of Virsylvia Peak (12,594 feet) and the sweeping alpine landscape. Both basins below you are decorated with small tarns, and easy slopes provide access to these and possible backcountry campsites. To the south, you can see the ski runs of Red River and portions of the Columbine-Hondo Wilderness Study Area.

Below Latir Peak, which is less than 0.5 mile to the north, lies a string of lakes arranged like polished stones on a silver bracelet. You can reach the Latir Lakes on a trail originating from the northeast, or by moving cross country below Latir Peak. From the saddle on which you're currently standing, the incredible highline run continues as the trail curls around the north side of a blocky rock outcropping to reach another saddle of sorts. There is a slow right-hand swing into a gentle, downsloping gully and a cross-slope run. The way continues to be marked by rock cairns and stretches of recognizable game-like trails.

From the second saddle you reach a cairn at 7.3 miles. Look downslope or down the gully to spot the next cairn and the route. There is a signed junction for Rito del Medo at approximately 7.6 miles. Continue cross-slope just above the tree line. The trail here is much more visible, and it makes an easy, beautiful run to the junction with the Bull Creek Trail and Cabresto Peak at 7.9 miles. Stop a moment to take it all in because from here you leave the phenomenal and glorious highline exposure and sink back into the sights, sounds, and rhythms of the forest.

The trail drops down a couloir and reaches a small campsite and the beginnings of Bull Creek at 8.2 miles. It makes a very nice run through the forest with a number of creek crossings. Lush riparian zones host tall yellow and purple flowers growing en masse. At 9.9 miles, you enter a small clearing with views of a couple rocky highpoints nearby. Shortly thereafter you cross over Bull Creek. The trail continues its pleasant slide downslope, passing close to the confluence of Lagunitas and Bull Creeks before crossing over Bull to reach the junction with the Heart Lake Trail at 10.5 miles. From here, retrace your steps back to the trailhead and parking area to complete the 13-mile hike.

Wild New Mexico

As it stands today, New Mexico has 24 wilderness areas totaling some 1.6 million acres, which is only 2 percent of the land. The Gila Wilderness in the southwest corner of the state is the largest at 558,065 acres. The smallest is Dome Wilderness at 5,200 acres. The Pecos Wilderness is the largest in northern New Mexico at 222,673 acres. There are more than 35 areas classified as wilderness study areas across the state. Currently five of these are up for consideration by Congress for wilderness status.

33

Placer Creek to Gold Hill Loop

Type: Overnight

Season: June to October

Total distance: 16 miles

Rating: Moderate to strenuous

Elevation gain: 5,000 feet

Location: Carson National Forest, 14 miles north of Taos

Maps: USGS Questa and Red River

Getting There

From Taos, take NM 522 approximately 25.5 miles north to the town of Questa. The junction for NM 38 is at the stoplight in Questa. Turn right, or east, toward Red River. Look for Columbine Campground on the right 5.2 miles (27.7 miles total) down NM 38. The campground road circles around to a small parking lot beside the trailhead. If you are coming from Red River, it is approximately 7 miles to the campground.

The Trail

Gold Hill can be seen as the shorter, younger, and less popular brother to Wheeler Peak (Hike 34). But a down-the-boulevard view into the Williams Lake basin, vistas over the Cimarron Range, and close-up takes into the Latir Wilderness and beyond allow Gold Hill to compete with its older sibling any day of week. When you add in the approach up Placer Creek into the secluded Willow Creek basin and the slide across the grassy ridgebacks leading to the summit of Gold Hill, this experience may even exceed Wheeler's adventure and aesthetics.

The hike begins on Columbine Creek Trail 71, which runs along the creek of the same name. It crosses over three times via arcing footbridges on its way up a wide drainage toward the central ridgeline that runs through the 30,500-acre Columbine-Hondo Wilderness Study Area. Highpoints here include Lobo Peak (12,115 feet) and nearly a half-dozen others in the 12,000-foot range.

The highest protection for a special area and the creatures that inhabit it would be a refuge that restricts all human entry. The next level is a designated wilderness area, which allows low-impact human ac-

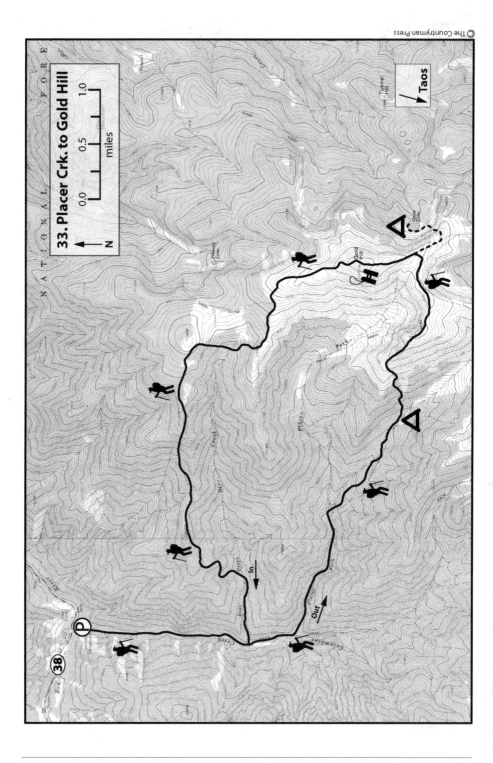

cess but restricts potentially destructive practices like logging, mining, and, in most cases, grazing. Wilderness study areas like the one through which you are hiking can be thought of as leading candidates for wilderness area status. There is a wide range of benefits in allowing nature to maintain its own balance. And restricting resource extraction operations and mechanized travel in these special places also keeps new roads from being built.

You don't actually reach the central ridgeline on this hike, as you deviate up a different creek drainage to the east far before then. It is definitely an adventure, not a crazy one, but surely different from the maintained feel of more popular trails. You will hike up along the overgrown but very manageable Placer Creek Trail into a brilliant two-tiered basin that leads farther on to a fantastic highline run up to the summit of Gold Hill.

The first 1 mile along Columbine Creek is an open zone with aspen and fir trees and a mix of wildflowers that includes the area's namesake, the Colorado columbine. The large bloom has five pointy petals circling five cylinders, painted in a soft bluish-purple blended with ivory white. Columbine typically blooms by July. The first skip over the creek comes at 0.4 mile. Apparently wanting to show off each side of the creek equally, the trail makes another crossing at 0.6 mile and then at 0.9 mile—thimbleberry and wild raspberry bushes line portions of the trail along here—before reaching the junction with the Columbine-Twinning National Recreation Trail at 1.5 miles. This will be the return trail for our hike.

So even though the sign indicates that Gold Hill is to the left, continue straight along the Columbine Creek Trail toward Lobo Peak. You cross the creek again shortly past the junction and continue through similar riparian vegetation. At 3 miles you reach the Placer Creek junction. Head left, crossing Columbine Creek yet again, to begin working your way up this rarely visited drainage.

The trail can be overgrown, but it is quite easy to navigate, with numerous crossings of Placer Creek and a jungle path through a lush riparian zone and aspen groves. At 4.3 miles the trail makes a few slightly wider swings away from the creek and starts to angle more steeply uphill in a more open setting. At 4.8 miles, you reach the junction of Placer Creek and Willow Fork (also signed for Gold Hill). Take the Willow Creek Trail, which heads to the right, making one last crossing of Placer Creek. At the junction or just a little beyond along the Willow Fork, you will find a nice clearing in which to set up camp if you so desire.

A beautiful grove of aspen appears at 5.4 miles, and the forest floor is carpeted with thick grass and wildflowers. The trail is consumed somewhat by the setting so make sure you just maintain your course, not gaining or losing elevation, for approximately 50 yards before it shows itself again. The section of trail from the last junction has become more strenuous. In another 0.2 mile (5.6 miles total) you reach a similar aspen zone where the trail again can be difficult to follow. This time you cross an expanse of about 80 yards to pick up the trail.

At 5.9 miles you enter a small meadow where you must move through the wide-spaced trees near the edge in order to stay on the trail. At 6.3 miles you enter the bottom end of a fantastic basin. The headwaters of Willow Creek carve a line through this open grass and wildflower zone. Trees are thickly gathered along the

Gold Hill looming above tree line

south wall of the basin, as well as leading up to the ridge. There are great views of Flag Mountain (11,946 feet) to the west. This is an ideal location for an overnight campsite.

From here to the top of the basin, the route can be a little tricky, but don't be deterred. As you always should, just make sure to carry a good topographic map and compass. Move up through the lower basin along the creek, following a faint trail. If you lose the trail, just remember to follow the main creek more to the north. This leads you to the upper basin, which is decorated with large mounds of earth, at 6.8 miles. A side drainage cuts along the gentler slope to the left, and a trail takes you up toward the north rim of the basin. Once you're on the backbone of the

ridge/rim, a trail leads to a cairn and post marking the highpoint and a picture-perfect view of Gold Hill to the east.

Move more toward the east to reach a trail (7.4 miles) that straddles the basin you just climbed out of and the beautiful Placer Fork basin set 500 feet below to the east. After climbing a ramp-like section of trail, you reach the highpoint on the east side of the basin. A cairn and fenceline mark the junction to Gold Hill at 7.8 miles. Be aware that the next 2 miles or so of this hike are above tree line, which can leave you exposed to lightning. Always watch for thunderstorms. Looking east, Gold Hill is the highest point. The trail that leads to Gold Hill runs down the near slope. Covering a distance of 0.4 mile (8.2 miles total), the trail reaches an area of patchy trees. It's

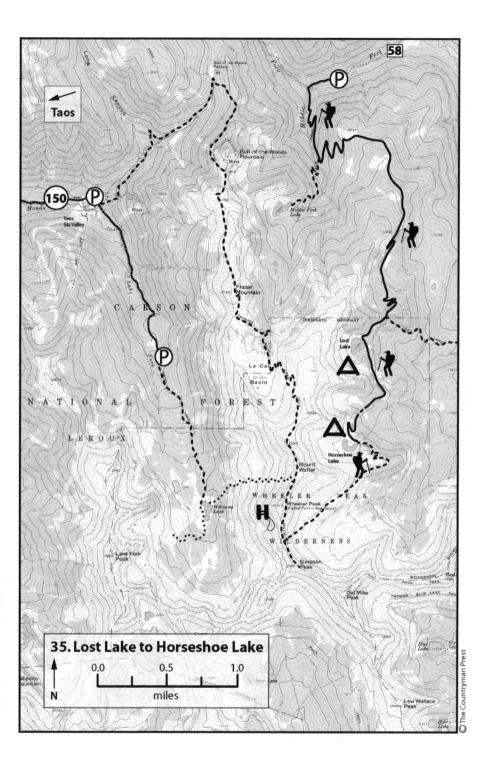

35. Lost Lake to Horseshoe Lake

0.0   0.5   1.0

miles

N

The valleys are tight and tall as you walk the 0.2 mile to the bridge crossing of the West Fork and begin the steep ascent up the thickly forested Middle Fork drainage. You twist up six switchbacks on the east side of the drainage along an old road before reaching a trail junction at 1.3 miles.

Tucked into a nook in the ridgeline to the west, Middle Fork Lake is accessed by continuing straight at the junction. The route to Lost Lake and Horseshoe Lake follows a switchback ascent up the east side of the creek drainage along a hiker's trail. At 2.7 miles, the trail begins to make a slow bend from east to south. To the west, you have nice views of Bull-of-the-Woods Mountain (11,514 feet), Frazer Mountain (12,163 feet) farther to the south, and other features of the first section of the highline run for Wheeler Peak (accessed from the Taos Ski Valley).

The trees are spaced wider apart through here as you continue to gain elevation, although much more gradually. The trail follows a finger ridge that eventually leads along the bottom end of a steep-walled mountain jetty of sorts attached to the Wheeler Peak and Mount Walter ridgeline. This also forms the eastern wall of the La Cal Basin. Open rockslide slopes are colored in yellow groundsel and out below the run you have views over the wide Moreno Valley, which is edged by the Cimarron Range rising some 4,000 feet above the valley floor.

The trail alternates between tree cover and open slope, first to the East Fork Trail junction (4.2 miles) and then along the short run up to Lost Lake at 4.7 miles. You officially enter the Wheeler Peak Wilderness shortly before the lake. Lost is a small lake horseshoed by trees. Its western shoreline runs into a rocky slope dropping from a 12,400-foot ridgeline. There are

plenty of campsites on the north and south sides of the lake. Just be mindful to not trample the vegetation.

The journey connecting Lost Lake to Horseshoe Lake is a short one. You gain about 600 vertical feet in 1 mile, mainly in the trees, and then tackle a couple of switchbacks. There are tent sites at the top of the last switchback, just before you step onto a huge open slope where Horseshoe Lake is the blue gem in a world of green (5.7 miles). The trail crosses over the lake's outlet and works up the rocky southeast corner of the basin to a benched area stippled with trees. This makes for an excellent high camp with views of Wheeler Peak as well as the protection of the trees. In 2006, a helicopter crash-landed on this bench during a search-and-rescue operation (pilot and passengers survived).

This area leads into a ridgeback ascent and then a beautiful, long arcing trail that bisects the east slope of Wheeler Peak. It aims for the mountain's south shoulder and the final approach to the summit. The slope, which forms one wall of another giant basin, is a collection of thick clumps of green grasses, flowering shrubs, and a virtual garden of wildflowers like lupine, paintbrush, cinquefoil, and many other vibrant varieties.

Two tarns are set in the bottom of the basin. And there is the possibility of meeting up with a healthy population of Rocky Mountain bighorn sheep as you make your cross-slope journey. It is about 0.7 mile from Horseshoe Lake to the ridgeback that leads to the broad slope. In another 0.8 mile, you move onto another ridgeline, this one connecting Simpson Peak and Wheeler Peak. Heading north (left), you finish the last 0.4 mile to the summit of Wheeler Peak. Here you can see another

Beautiful Lost Lake

Lost Lake to Horseshoe Lake

amazing basin and high-peak overlook to the west, along with a whole collection of other visual treats in the Truchas Peaks to the south and the Gold Hill area to the north. This is indeed a marvelous outing. The climb up and back from Wheeler Peak adds 3.8 miles to the hiking distance, making the total 15.2 miles.

East Fork Red River Alternative

This trail brings you by an old relic of the mining days in the Elizabethtown Ditch, which carried water from the mountains out across the Moreno Valley (a distance of 41 miles). The setting is similar to the West Fork approach except that the trail more closely shadows the creek drainage (the East Fork this time). This trail adds about 1.5 miles of total distance to the hike to Horseshoe Lake.

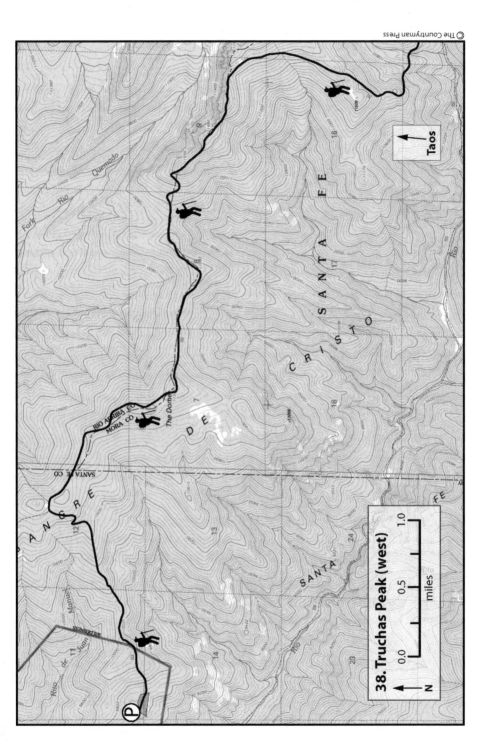

Taos

38. Truchas Peak (West)

miles

0.0   0.5   1.0

N

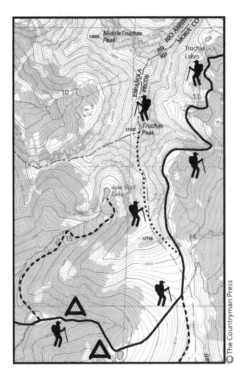

© The Countryman Press

made up of North (13,024 feet), Middle (13,066 feet), and Truchas (13,102 feet). Truchas is known by local Pueblo people as Stone Man Mountain. The trail drops and rises in easily digestible amounts, reaching a distinctive highpoint at 4.2 miles before dropping steeply to a cross-slope run. At 4.4, miles you reach a small clearing in the trees. One trail continues straight and another heads to the right. Follow the trail to the right, paying attention to the tree blazes through the next short, somewhat difficult-to-follow stretch.

Soon after the clearing, the trail climbs 0.5 mile before flattening out and moving cross slope. By 5.2 miles, you are rewarded with your first big views of the Truchas Peaks. The west slopes are steep and lead into deep, tall basins, one of which cradles Jose Vigil Lake. The trail drops into and over the creek drainage to meet the Jose Vigil Trail junction at 6.6 miles. A steep climb of 1.2 miles brings you up into the Jose Vigil Lake basin. No camping is allowed in the basin itself.

To continue on the route to Truchas Peak, go straight. After losing some elevation, you meet Trail 351 at 7.1 miles. Take the trail to the left as it passes through a narrow meadow with campsites and then follows a creek up to a more open, circular meadow with a tarn set in the middle, another campsite option. From here the trail moves to the north, making a 0.7-mile push out of the trees and onto the spectacular north end of the Trailriders Wall (8.3 miles).

Trying to consume all the views that surround you in this open zone will make you dizzy—the Truchas Peaks in your face to the north, the spread of the Pecos Wilderness to the east, and East Pecos Baldy tethered to the Trailriders Wall to the south. You have two options at this point: head to the

strenuous ascent at 0.8 mile and continuing to a trail junction at 1.6 miles. Heading right puts you on Trail 151 toward The Dome (11,336 feet) along a much less strenuous route. Views of the mountains across the broad Rio Medio drainage are possible through the trees along here. The forest understory is sparse, occasionally broken up by a wildflower or mushroom cap that adds color and character to the forest floor. The moderate climb lasts until the 2.4-mile mark, where you begin a steeper ascent toward The Dome. At 2.7 miles there is a fork in the trail. Stay to the right as the trail loses a little elevation before moving cross-slope just slightly below the summit of The Dome.

In between the aspen trees along this stretch, you begin to have glimpses of East Pecos Baldy (12,529 feet) and the Truchas Peaks. The Truchas Peaks are

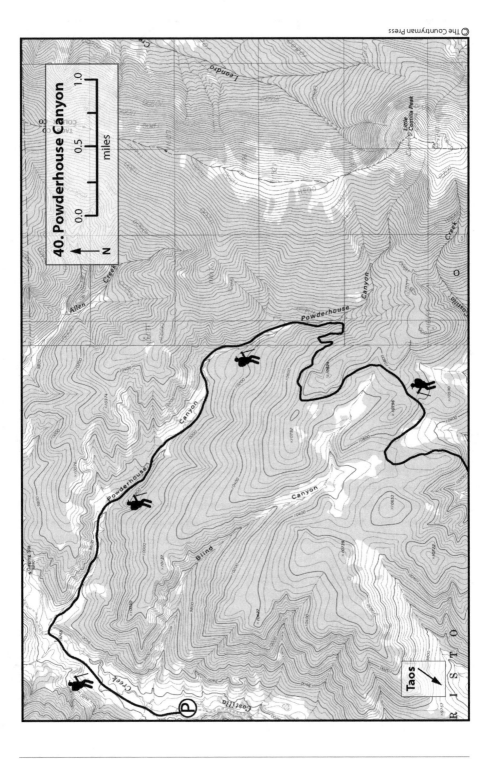

40. Powderhouse Canyon

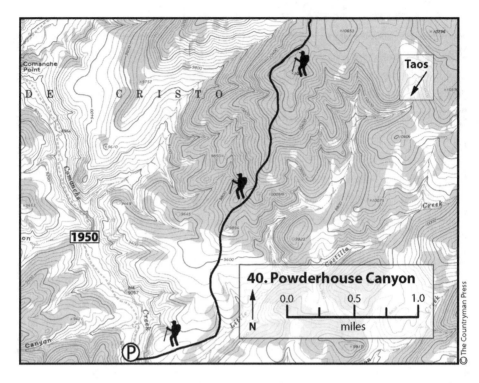

straight you would reach a gate and a NO TRESPASSING sign.

You may notice, as you pass through this short valley, that a lush riparian ecosystem feeds off the constant moisture of the creek. But a short distance beyond this swath, the plant life changes to a more semi-arid mix of wildflowers and bushes. After crossing the creek, the road makes a gentle bend to the right and reaches a gate at 1 mile. This marks the entry into Powderhouse Canyon. On the other side of a dam lies Costilla Reservoir and the 580,000-acre Vermejo Ranch.

Powderhouse Canyon begins as a shallow, grassy valley, narrower than the Upper Costilla valley. It soon constricts, though, and you'll notice the trees slipping closer to the creek and road as you move up valley. The area of the Valle Vidal ("Valley of Life" in Spanish) was roamed by hunter-

gatherers as far back as 10,000 years. These people, known as Folsom people because of artifacts found near Folsom, New Mexico, were the ancestors of early Anazazi people who eventually spread across many regions of the Southwest. Today hikers wander the Valle Vidal in part by way of abandoned roads instead of trails. The hundreds of miles of roadway have a history in mining and timber operations, but their presence won't lessen the aesthetic beauty of the journey.

It is possible in the lower valleys, and even more likely as you head deeper into the hike, that you will encounter numerous elk. The countryside along the Valle Vidal is ideal elk habitat, with numerous open spaces, wide-spaced trees, and terrain that varies from rolling hills to steeper slopes leading up to highpoints like Little Costilla Peak (12,584 feet).

The Valle Vidal holds many treasures.

At 2 miles, you come to a road that splits off to the left. A small shack sits on the other side of the creek here, along with a water-control gate. Continue straight along the creek. Turn around at this point for a nicely framed view of the rugged Big Costilla Peak (12,739 feet) and ridgeline. Shortly past here you move above the creek and through more of a corridor of trees, marking the transition from valley to forest travel.

At 3 miles, you cross over the creek and enter a more open zone of the drainage, climbing a bit more as you go. You pass by two roads that cut off to the right before reaching a third such road at 3.5 miles. There is no sign here, although it may be marked by a cairn, but you'll recognize this spot because you will see a road making its way up the slope on the opposite side of

the creek. Follow this road to the right for approximately 0.2 mile (3.7 miles total) to a creek crossing. If you happen to continue straight at this junction instead of heading to the right, you will reach another fork. Here the road continuing straight crosses over a faint, slightly overgrown road and the one to the left climbs steeply for a short stretch. If you reach this point you've made a mistake and need to turn around and make your way back to the left fork at the previous junction.

After crossing the creek, the old road winds its way up the near slope and out and around a highpoint. This area was heavily logged in the early to mid-20th century. Approximately 0.2 mile up there is another split in the road; stay to the right. Along here, and for most of the remaining hike, you have different takes on Little Costilla Peak. The scars of old logging roads are still somewhat visible on its western slope, but today it's thickly treed up to around 11,700 feet. The last 800 feet or so are treeless. Elk encounters, especially if you are out early, are very likely along much of the rest of this hike.

By 4.2 miles, you reach a clearing of sorts and an intersection of logging roads. There are nice views across the Valle Vidal. The hike follows the road as it bends to the left and back into a corridor of trees. The road follows a curving ridgeline for 3.5 miles, sometimes walled in by trees and sometimes through clearings that provide views of Little Costilla as well as Tetilla Peak (10,600 feet) and Van Diest Peak (11,223 feet) off to the left, or south.

You have an easy glide for a number of miles before descending gradually back to the main valley floor. At 4.7 miles the road bends away from Little Costilla, but in its place there is a beautiful overlook of a lush meadow, an ideal location for a campsite. Another clearing and road intersection come at 5 miles. Stay on the road that makes a gentle bend to the right, which is noticeably the more traveled route. At 5.8 miles, there is a nice mix of forest and meadow, an ideal place to do a little exploring off the main path if you are feeling up to it.

The road already has met up with clearings at various points, and another arrives at 6.5 miles. Little Costilla puts on another worthy face from this vantage point, and the route stays straight before bending to the left and entering a more treed section. A broad open slope, dotted occasionally with trees, hangs like a landscape canvas across the drainage of a tributary that feeds Little Costilla Creek. There also are opening views of the eastern and northeastern slopes of the Cimarron Range.

After a promenade along the northeastern edge of the Valle Vidal, cut by Comanche Creek in the distance, the road turns once again toward Little Costilla at 7.6 miles. After a 0.4-mile stretch, the views return to the long gentle rolling valley, with the Cimarron Range as backdrop. In another 0.3 mile (8.3 miles total), you have walked by your last serious covering of trees—ponderosa pine instead of the previous aspen and fir—and are now in the expansive valley.

At 9.2 miles you reach FS 1950 and your shuttle vehicle. No shuttle vehicle? From here it is 5.5 miles back to the Powderhouse trailhead. If you would prefer to make this hike as an out-and-back, it will be much more engaging and scenic to start from this trailhead instead of the Powderhouse trailhead.

"Life Giving" Valley Holding on for Dear Life

The Valle Vidal (*vidal* means "life giving" in Spanish) was donated to the American people by the Penzoil Corporation in 1982. Its 101,794 acres, managed by the Carson National Forest, were set aside so that hikers, horsemen, cross-country skiers, hunters, and anglers could enjoy this truly unique landscape. A 40,000-acre area has been coveted by mining interests for oil and natural gas extraction. But the Coalition for the Valle Vidal was formed by concerned citizens, businesses, and conservation groups like the Sierra Club to put a stop to any notions of violating the natural beauty of the Valle Vidal for short-term gains. As of November 2006, the Valle Vidal Protection Act to restrict all mining speculation and operations here has passed through both the House and Senate and is awaiting signed approval from the President. Stay connected to all the issues concerning the Valle Vidal by visiting www.vallevidal.com.

41

Clayton Camp

Type: Day hike

Season: June to November

Total distance: 3.4 miles

Rating: Moderate

Elevation gain: 100 feet

Location: Valle Vidal, 35 miles north-northeast of Taos

Maps: USGS Comanche Point

Getting There

From Taos, drive 45 miles north on NM 522, passing through Questa, to the town of Costilla and the junction for NM 196. Turn right onto NM 196. At 55.7 miles, the road transitions from pavement to dirt and gravel, and it's now marked as FS 1950. Approximately 8 miles (63.6 miles) along FS 1950, you reach a fork in the road. FS 1900 is straight ahead, but you stay to the right, continuing on FS 1950. In approximately 4.2 miles, you reach a road that splits off to the right just before FS 1950 starts to climb. At 0.4 mile down this unsigned road (68.2 miles total), you reach a small parking area and a gate across the road.

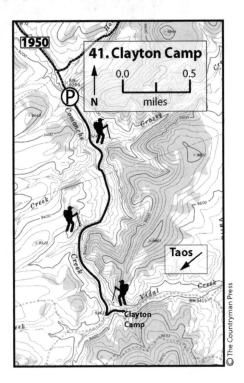

Clayton Camp

The Trail

The Valle Vidal is in recovery. Heavy logging and devastating grazing practices—6,000 head of cattle ran at times in some areas—have damaged streamside habitats. But volunteers are working to restore a natural balance so native species like the Rio Grande cutthroat trout can thrive again. A major restoration project is under way along Comanche Creek, led by the Quivira Coalition. The hike to Clayton Camp edges along that creek, making this journey about the future and the past.

Comanche Creek moves quietly through this small, shallow canyon. There are interesting rock formations near the beginning of the hike and nice collections of grasses and wildflowers the entire way.

Approximately 0.8 mile down, you cross the creek and pass through a gate. The creek bottom terrain also opens up through here into more of a dry grass environment. There are plenty of opportunities all along this hike to strike out across the rolling valley or head up into more forested sections. By 1.3 miles, the road has made a bend to the left, crossed the creek again, and entered a narrower valley bottom. You reach Clayton Camp at 1.7 miles.

You pass a small stock pen and outbuilding before coming upon the main house. This point also marks the confluence of Comanche and Vidal Creeks. With a map and compass, you could continue on by exploring either creek drainage. Aster, giant thistle, cinquefoil, tiny daises, and scarlet gilia paint the ground.

44

Clear Creek Canyon

Type: Day hike

Season: June to October

Total distance: 5 miles

Rating: Moderate

Elevation gain: 950 feet

Location: Cimarron Canyon State Park, 25 miles northeast of Taos

Maps: USGS Touch-Me-Not Mountain

Getting There

From Taos, take US 64 east 34.5 miles to the town of Eagle Nest. Continue east on US 64 through town, heading toward Cimarron Canyon State Park. At 37.2 miles, you reach the park entrance, as well as the Colin Neblett Wildlife Management Area. Stop at the park office on the left to pay the $5-per-vehicle, day-use fee. From the park boundary, continue another 6 miles (43.2 miles total) to a small parking area on the right just past a big bend in the road. Because the parking area arrives unexpectedly, it helps to watch for the Ferryville day-use area about a mile before the turn on the opposite side of the road.

The Trail

Often overlooked by hikers, the Cimarron Canyon is probably the most rugged

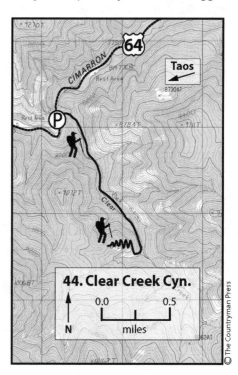

44. Clear Creek Cyn.

0.0   0.5

N   miles

© The Countryman Press

mountain landscape in northern New Mexico. The Cimarron Range runs along the eastern edge of the gorgeous Eagle Nest valley. Its highpoint, Baldy Mountain (12,441 feet), stands some 4,000 feet above the gentle valley bottom. Bisecting the range is the Cimarron River, running through a narrow, extremely steep, forested canyon. Marvelously sculpted cliffs muscle free of the thick forest, the most impressive being the Palisade cliff band, which measures some 200 feet in height. Cottonwoods shade the river, giving cover and life to a wonderful 8-mile stretch of trout fishing. Occasionally the canyon relents and reveals passages up one side or the other for deeper exploration of this backcountry gem.

Clear Creek spills down from Mount Phillips (11,741 feet), slipping by groves of aspen and thick stands of fir, down natural waterslides, and over rock ledges in elegant waterfalls. The trail stays along the creek nearly the entire time, crossing from one side to the other. Then it takes a right turn up a side drainage to gain a highpoint and an overview across the Cimarron Canyon and into the trailless backcountry to the south.

Cimarron Canyon State Park is small, primarily clinging to the area around the Cimarron River and a few side canyons. It is set inside a 33,116-acre area known as the Colin Neblett Wildlife Management Area, the largest such area in New Mexico. The rugged terrain and lack of trail access make it ideal for healthy populations of deer, elk, and wild turkey.

From the parking area, walk the road to the east and cross over Clear Creek near its confluence with the Cimarron River to reach a sign for the Clear Creek Trail. A somewhat rocky trail, this setting is meant for strolling. You pass through a fir forest

decorated here and there by aspen and move along creekside communities of Gamble oak, alder, wild rose, wild raspberry, harebell, aster, phlox, cinquefoil, and wild strawberry. By 0.9 mile the trail has crossed the creek four times via footlog, moved above the creek for a stretch, and passed the first waterfall.

At 1.5 miles, with the trail up from the creek, a side trail moves down to an observation point for a second waterfall that moves across a natural rock waterslide. The canyon begins to open up around this point, even though you're still in tree cover. Shortly after the second waterfall, the trail meets another beautiful water feature. Here the creek drops and slides for about 50 feet into a series of pools. The trail crosses above this area, then moves by some pointed rock outcroppings and through a lush riparian zone.

The trail makes a turn away from Clear Creek at the 2-mile mark to begin the viewpoint climb. The last 0.5 mile is a strenuous push up a snaking, loose rock trail that moves along a finger ridge. Down to the left is a wide, long swath of aspen that appears as a massive bar of gold in the autumn. The highpoint is reached at 2.5 miles. Across the Cimarron Canyon are rugged, steep slopes, the forest interrupted here and there by rocky patches and outcroppings. Up the Clear Creek drainage, the steep slopes are thick with fir trees. This outing is well worth it for its own sake, but also in contrast to other subapline zones in northern New Mexico.

Bottoms Up!

There are only four designated trails—less than 15 miles—in the entire park and wildlife area. They each start from the canyon bottom and move up steep

The Cimarron Range

drainages along the Cimarron River. The Jasper and Agate Trails and the Maverick Canyon Trail are up canyon. At the mouth of the canyon, just outside Eagle Nest, is the Tolby Creek Canyon Trail, which offers a great overlook of the Eagle Nest valley. No backcountry camping is allowed—a preservation measure to protect this place for wildlife.

45

Capulin Volcano

Type: Day hike

Season: April to November

Total distance: 1 mile

Rating: Moderate

Elevation gain: 275 feet

Location: Capulin Volcano National Monument, 25 miles east of Raton

Maps: USGS Folsom

Getting There

From Raton, take US 64/87 for 29 miles to the town of Capulin. Turn left onto NM 325 toward the Capulin Volcano National Monument. At 32.7 miles (2.7 miles from the junction), take a right into the entrance for the national monument. There is a visitor center a short distance into the park where you can stop for information and to pay the entry fee—$5 per vehicle, valid for seven days of access. Continue on the winding road toward the top to reach another parking area at 34.8 miles.

The Trail

The eruptions that formed the Capulin Volcano some 60,000 years ago came in the third phase of volcanic development, which took place over a period of 9 million years. Even though there is a calm about this area today, giant bison and mammoths once roamed the wispy grasslands that radiate out in all directions. And bursts of fiery ash, miles of fast-flowing lava, and sky-shattering explosions were all part of the scene at various times. Today the Capulin Volcano is a natural pyramid, a pristine example of a cinder cone rarely seen in this country.

There are two ways to explore the extinct volcano. The first is a 1-mile rim trail that provides 360-degree views of the surrounding geography and four distinct lava flows that move out from the volcano's base. The second is a short trail that leads into the bottom of the volcano, next to where the vent became plugged by cooling lava. Capulin came under federal protection in 1891, very early in the conservation movement, and received national monument status in 1916 under President Wilson.

The paved rim trail is lined with a col-

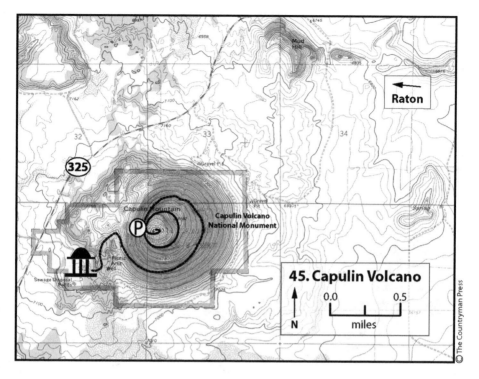

45. Capulin Volcano

0.0   0.5

N   miles

lection of vegetation from Gamble oak and mahogany to juniper and a variety of wild-flowers. Chokecherry bushes—the berries edible fresh, in jams, or dried—also grow on Capulin. In fact, the word *capulin* means chokecherry in Spanish. As you probably noticed on the drive up to the parking area and again while circling the rim, the volcano has extremely steep slopes all around. The materials that make up the volcano are loose cinders, ash, and other rock debris brought up from deep underground during its eruption. The vegetation blanketing Capulin today has been key in stabilizing the fragile slopes.

Starting on the south side of the rim trail, you can look down on what are labeled the third and second lava flows. These are followed by the first lava flow, which comes off the southeast side of the volcano. The fourth lava flow, the largest, moved northward. All told they cover nearly 16 square miles. An interesting feature of the flows are the ripples that formed as the crust cooled with hotter lava still flowing underneath. Lava mounds formed when building pressure split the not-yet-hardened crust and lava bubbled up.

Sierra Grande (8,720 feet), the bulky flat-topped highpoint you can see to the southeast, is classified as a shield volcano. Shield volcanoes are built by highly fluid spreads of lava that create broad, gently sloped mountains. Mesas like Barilla, Raton, and Johnson and other highpoints dot the landscape in each direction. This area, covering some 8,000 square miles, is known as the Raton-Clayton Volcanic Field. Looking west, the long wall of 12,000-foot peaks running north to south is the Sangre de Cristo Mountains. There is much on which to ruminate as you circle the rim, and

Capulin Volcano

this hike will most likely spur you to learn more about this region of New Mexico. But looking inward can do the same.

A trail dropping from the parking lot leads to an observation point in the crater bottom. Gamble oak has settled in this zone and grass coats the inside walls, with pinion pine and juniper frosting the upper reaches. This is the point where the volcano was born, creating a 1,300-plus-foot mountain where nothing existed before in the blink of an eye. The only activity today can be seen and heard in the bird chatter, the scurry and chirp of ground squirrels, and the movement of deer foraging for food.

Human Flow

Off the east side of Capulin runs what is known as the Fort Union–Grande Road. Fort Union has gone through three different manifestations; what stands today was constructed in the 1860s. The fort was conceived by General Stephen Watts Kearny, and later followed through on by Colonel Edwin V. Sumner in 1851. Its mission was to protect area communities and travelers along the Santa Fe Trail from hostile tribes over a 40-year period. Its presence and defensive layout also helped thwart an attack by Texas Confederates in 1861. Fort Union is located between Las Vegas and Wagon Mound and is now a national monument. Granda, Colorado, is 200 miles away. The two northern routes of the Santa Fe Trail that converged on Fort Union are the Cimarron Cutoff, which moved to the south of Capulin and on into Oklahoma, and the Mountain Branch, which moved through the present-day town of Raton and then north into Colorado. The two trails passed through Kansas to reach Kansas City, Missouri, a distance of 800 miles from Fort Union.

46

Aztec Ruins

Type: Day hike

Season: Year-round

Total distance: Less than 0.3 mile

Rating: Easy

Elevation gain: 10 feet

Location: Aztec Ruins National Monument, 12 miles northeast of Farmington

Maps: USGS Aztec

Getting There

From Farmington, take NM 516 east toward the town of Aztec. A couple of signs for Aztec Ruins precede the turn onto Ruins Road at 12 miles. In a short 0.6 mile, you reach the parking area and visitor center. Admission is $5 per person, and a National Parks Pass is accepted.

The Trail

The Aztec Ruins were just that—ruins—before the excavation from 1916 to 1921, managed by Earl Morris. Much of the building complex had been filled in or destroyed by blowing sand, the natural collapse of rock walls, and acts of vandalism. Yet what is known today as the West Ruin has been restored enough that many walls of the 400 rooms—three stories high at points in the complex—are clearly visible above ground on the small rise along the Animas River. This ancient site was known by area residents, relatives of the Aztec Pueblo people, and then Spanish and white settlers, and it was often visited with out-of-town guests or for amateur archeological explorations. Until Morris's work, it wasn't known what the former community of 1,000 people, dating back to the 1100s, really looked like. Its physical layout eventually was revealed and thousands of artifacts surfaced to help explain daily lives of the earliest inhabitants, including how they honored the dead.

After the mysterious demise of the Chaco Canyon pueblos, people migrated out across the area in two different directions. One group headed west, creating a society in what is today Canyon de Chelly National Monument in Arizona. Other families headed north, settling in the present-day Four Corners area. An extensive community thrived in Hovenweep in Utah,

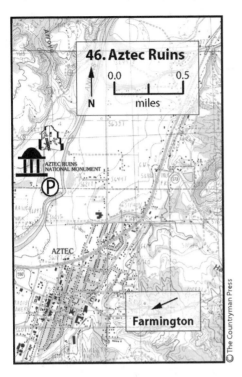

46. Aztec Ruins

↑ N

0.0   0.5
⊢————⊣
miles

AZTEC RUINS
NATIONAL MONUMENT

Ⓟ

AZTEC

Farmington ←

© The Countryman Press

to show what things may have actually looked like when this community was thriving. At its height, somewhere between 700 and 1,000 people lived at the Aztec Ruins, subsisting like the generations before them by hunting and gathering and farming corn, beans, and squash. Much remains to be excavated in the 320-acre monument, including what is called the East Ruin and a number of mounds, but many fascinating items were uncovered during the West Ruin dig, everything from woven mats and blinds of willow to fine pottery and stone tools. Many of these objects can be seen today in the small museum inside the visitor center.

Even though the Aztec people had no actual association with this place, the name has stayed. To the ancestral Puebloan people this place may have just been known as "A Place by Flowing Waters." Its greatest advantage over a place like Chaco Canyon is its location next to a reliable water source in the Animas River. Timbers used in the construction of Aztec, like Chaco Canyon, came from forested zones up in Colorado, meaning that logs were carried 20 miles or more without the aid of beasts of burden. This site was mysteriously abandoned in 1300, with the next migration of Pueblo people heading southeast along the Rio Grande from the area of present-day Taos to around Albuquerque. Descendents of these early migrants still reside in the various active pueblos today.

Salmon in New Mexico?
South of Aztec you will find the town of Bloomfield and the Salmon Ruins. Constructed during the same time period as the Aztec Ruins, the Salmon Pueblo also consisted of great buildings—up to 300 and three stories high—and kivas. And the

as well as in the incredible cliffside cities of Mesa Verde in Colorado. In New Mexico, evidence of the human presence during this period remains in the Salmon and Aztec Ruins.

The name of these ruins is, of course, a misnomer, although it's consistent with other tales of the Aztecs and their great king, Montezuma, having visited various places in New Mexico. Buildings began rising in A.D. 1110. Sandstone rock was shaped into blocks and augmented with mud chinking, and the internal walls were later coated in a mud plaster. There were incredible engineering feats in how corners joined together, and some rooms even had diagonal doorways. These masonry innovations came from Chaco Canyon's last period.

The West Ruin had 26 kivas, including the Great Kiva, which was reconstructed

A series of doorways at the Aztec Ruins

Aztec Ruins

people here lived similar lives to their neighbors at Aztec. The name comes from a late-1800s homesteader, George Salmon, whose still-visible home and outbuildings occupied the same ground as the abandoned pueblo. His family's presence helped preserve the Salmon Ruins by keeping vandals and treasure hunters away. The Salmon Ruins are open to the public. Visit www.salmonruins.com for more information.

47

Bisti Badlands

Type: Day hike

Season: April to November

Total distance: 4 miles (minimum)

Rating: Easy

Elevation gain: 50 feet

Location: Bisti Wilderness, 35 miles south of Farmington

Maps: USGS Alamo Mesa West, Alamo Mesa East, and Huerfano Trading Post SW

Getting There

The Bisti Wilderness is located south of Farmington off NM 371, or what is known as the Bisti Highway. The left turn onto CR 7297 comes at approximately 37 miles. Watch for the BISTI WILDERNESS sign approximately 0.25 mile before the turn. The wide, gravel road heads east for 2 miles to a signed junction. Turn left here and travel another 1 mile north, crossing over a wash to reach the small parking area on the other side (40 miles).

The Trail

Even if there was a trail system for the Bisti Wilderness, also known as Bisti or the Bisti Badlands, it would fail to do justice to how you should discover this fantastical world, which is like no other in New Mexico. The Bisti is perfect for aimless wandering, like water finding the path of least resistance. You will be in the midst of a stone garden—sandstone stems holding teetering stone mushroom caps at impossible, seemingly playful angles. A maze of side arroyos take you to surreal landscapes filled with rock towers, fossilized tree stumps, and marble-sized stones, which are splashed across the ground as if a child's bucket had been turned over. There also are mud mounds with a surface like cracked rhino skin and dusted in white, powdery gypsum.

The Bisti (3,946 acres) is an easy place to explore, but a good map and compass can be useful. Two washes come together at the start of the hike and later split, with the De-na-zin Wash bending more to the south and the Alamo Wash continuing nearly due east. The Alamo is the main route, and as long as you stay within the wash, or keep a sense of where it is when you're off exploring, it is difficult to get lost

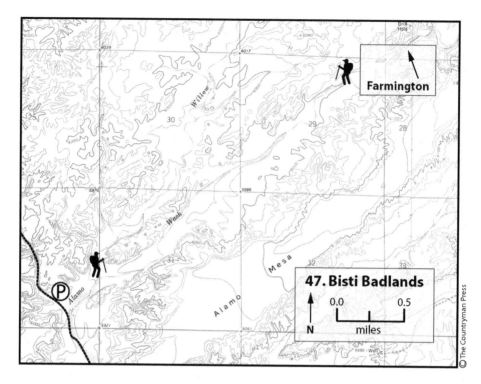

in the Bisti. When the weather is clear, you can see the Chuska Range some 37 miles to the west. These mountains are a good landmark for orienting yourself.

The various rock formations are the result of four different intervals of geologic history. This area is made up of what is known as Lewis Shale, which is more than 1,000 feet thick in locations within the San Juan Basin. One of the layers or intervals, the Fruitland Formation, is coal-bearing. The ocean was present here during all of these periods, and as it retreated the landscape was dominated by the surrounding mountains and the arid indentation of the San Juan Basin.

Spencer G. Lucas, in the book *Bisti*, writes about how this environment appeared in the beginning of the last geologic period where the sea was present with descriptions like, "Huge conifers...

towered above a jungle of ferns, palms, and other flowering plants," and "Horned dinosaurs...browsed unencumbered," and "the top of the terrestrial food chain rested solidly in the grasp of the enormous jaws of tyrannosaurid dinosaurs." Swamps, crocodiles, sharks, and clams were also part of this place some 100 million years ago.

The evidence of this surreal diversity is all around you in dinosaur bone fragments, the fossilized imprints of jungle plants, and numerous petrified tree stumps and sections up to 40 feet long. These will remind you of the existence of duckbilled dinosaurs and massive cypress trees. Water still moves through this stark, alien place from time to time, often in flash floods—water rushing along every possible channel to feed the central wash. Once-active rivulets are noticeable in the snake

Toadstool formations in the Bisti Badlands

belly–like imprints you see across the sandy ground. Water is surely scarce in the Bisti Badlands. Even so, a few small shrubs, tufts of grasses, and lonely wild-flowers have taken root along the wash.

Take time to enjoy the magic of the formations and think about the incredible transformations that have resulted over millions of years. To reach the heart of the sculpted features, you need to walk up the wash about 2 miles. There is still more to discover beyond this point, however, including channels that knife through tall dark clay hummocks. You can scramble on top of one of these for an overlook of this natural amusement park.

Bisti Coal Land

This name is not too far from the truth, evidenced by the mining operation just north of the Bisti Wilderness. An aerial overview of this region reveals the extensive and violent scarring of the landscape due to energy development. Those scars are the visible aspects of these operations, but the impacts go even farther, with groundwater pollution and the overuse of precious water. Thankfully, areas of geological, geographic, and cultural importance have been preserved within the Bisti Wilderness, but it also is important to preserve the surrounding landscape.

48

De-na-zin Wilderness

Type: Day hike

Season: April to November

Total distance: Variable

Rating: Moderate

Elevation gain: 100 feet

Location: De-na-zin Wilderness, 28 miles south-southeast of Farmington

Maps: USGS Alamo Mesa East and Huerfano Trading Post SW

Getting There

The Bisti Highway (NM 371) runs south from Farmington to reach the left turn onto CR 7500, the signed access to the De-na-zin Wilderness, in 44.6 miles. The road surface changes from pavement to packed dirt and it can be difficult to drive here after periods of heavy rain. Travel on CR 7500 for 13.3 miles (57.9 miles total) to a small, signed parking area on your left. It is also possible to access the wilderness from the east off US 550. From the junction of US 550 and CR 7500, it is 11.2 miles.

The Trail

The Bisti (Hike 47) and De-na-zin are actually one contiguous wilderness area, and have been since 1996, with a combined 47,800 acres. Connected they may be, but their environments and ecologies are quite different. The De-na-zin is a magical playground of unusual water- and wind-shaped sandstone formations set in the bottom of the broad De-na-zin Wash. Just like at Bisti, you will find blocky stone towers capped with teetering rocks and basketball-sized rocks perched on cutbanks, just waiting for the next heavy rain to send them tumbling. But the De-na-zin Wash has much more life in the collection of sage, cactus, yucca, juniper, pinion pine, chamisa, grasses, wildflowers, and tamarisk. With the plants come creatures like the bull snake, lizard, cottontail rabbit, jackrabbit, deer, and coyote.

From the parking area, follow the old Jeep road north toward the wash. Just before the road drops into the wash, a spur road branches off to the left to trace the rim through a sea of sage. This place is made for wandering, but one idea would be to explore the wash as far to the north

218   *50 Hikes in Northern New Mexico*

A rock city in the De-na-zin Wilderness

and west as you want and then loop back to the rim and along this rim road.

As with the Bisti, the Den-na-zin is defined by four distinct geologic periods. The most recent interval occurred some 70 million years ago. This last period was witness to the ebb and flow of oceans, swamps, and cypress trees, the fading of the dinosaur, and tectonic shifts that pushed forth mountain ranges and created the San Juan Basin. It is quite striking to imagine the ecology of this place millions of years ago compared to its present state of extremes—inhospitably intense summer heat and bitingly cold winter winds. This place was once a humid swamp environment with a massive cy-

press forest, and creatures like the armored ankylosaur and duckbilled hadrosaur foraged through the lush jungle foliage. It is quite common to find fossilized plants, petrified trees and tree stumps, and dinosaur fossils in the wash and along side channels.

Eskimos in the Desert

There is truth to this title in that the Apache tribe, of which the Navajo are part, have a link to the Athabaskan people of interior Alaska. The Navajo Diné language is considered Southern Athabaskan (there are 23 related Athabaskan languages), part of a 4,000-mile language link joined through tribes along coastal California and

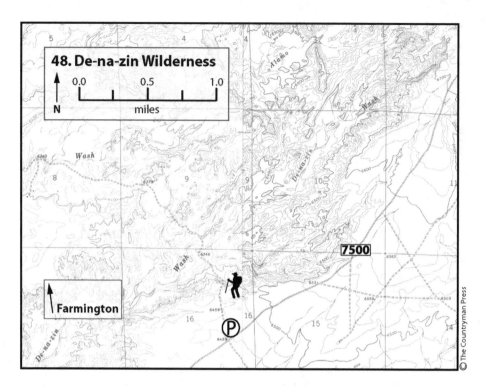

48. De-na-zin Wilderness

Oregon, as well as western Canada. The Athabaskan people are said to have made eastern and southern migrations from their homeland around A.D. 500. The Navajo people are said to have arrived in New Mexico sometime in the 1400s.

49

Peñasco Blanco

Type: Day hike

Season: April to November

Total distance: 7.1 miles

Rating: Moderate

Elevation gain: 200 feet

Location: Chaco Canyon National Historic Park, 48 miles south-southeast of Farmington

Maps: USGS Kin Klizhin Ruins and Pueblo Bonito

Getting There

From Farmington, travel 12 miles east on US 64 to the town of Bloomfield. Turn right onto US 550, heading south. At 39.2 miles down US 550, you reach the signed, right-hand turn for CR 7900. Plenty of signs along the way indicate the upcoming turn and deter you from taking other roads. In 5 miles (56.2 miles total), CR 7900 meets CR 7950, where you turn right onto CR 7950. Shortly after the turn 3 miles down, the road surface changes from pavement to packed dirt. The road can be difficult to navigate after heavy periods of rain. At 77.1 miles the road transitions from dirt to pavement again as you enter the outer boundary of the park. You pass by the campground before reaching the visitor center at 79.7 miles. The fee is $8 per vehicle, good for 7 days. The backcountry trail book you can obtain at the visitor center is quite handy to have on the hike, especially for explaining the various petroglyphs found along the way. Following the 8-mile loop road, you pass by Pueblo Bonito to the short spur road to reach the parking area directly across from Pueblo Arroyo (83.7 miles).

The Trail

The Chaco Wash was the fickle lifeblood of the Chacoan people during their 300 years here, gathering and delivering water only during the spring thaw and after heavy summer rains. Attempts were made to enhance a natural dam at the confluence of the Chaco and Escavado Washes, most likely to create some predictability in this precious resource for farming and everyday life. The Chaco Wash may not have water coursing through it when you hike to Peñasco Blanco, but it will provide access to two Great Houses, petroglyphs

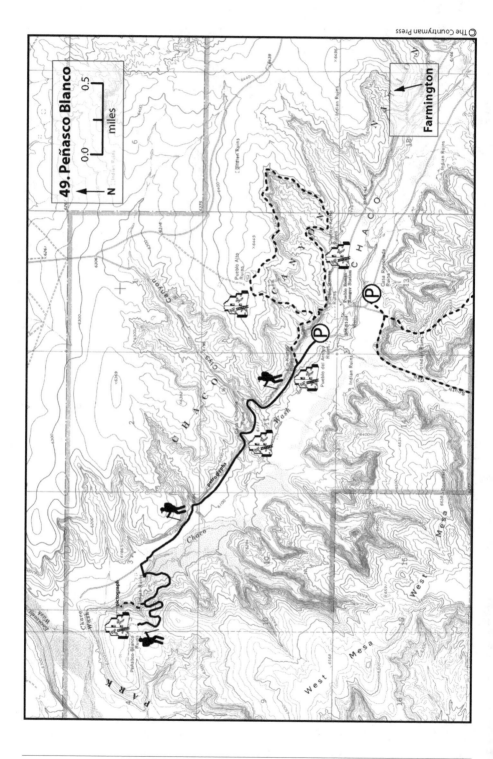

49. Peñasco Blanco

N

0.0   0.5

miles

Farmington

Peñasco Blanco

created by the people of Chaco and more recent works by the Navajos, a down-canyon view of the area from one of the more sacred sites of Chaco, and a record of astronomical history.

Kin Kletso is visible 0.2 mile down the roadway, which parallels the wash the entire way before crossing it for the climb up to Peñasco Blanco. Kin Kletso was built in A.D. 1130 and included 54 ground-level rooms. Behind the ruin is the trail access for New Alto and Pueblo Alto. Because of the wash, cottonwood trees pop up along the route, the largest concentration gathered by a bend in the wash near the crossing. The whole Chaco Canyon area is home primarily to grease bush, sagebrush, yucca, cactus, and rain-sparked wildflowers. Other flora species include sumac, Indian rice grass, Gamble oak, and chamisa.

At 0.9 mile, just after a hairpin bend, you arrive at Casa Chiquita. The landscape appears to be slowly swallowing up the squat structure. Like most of the pueblos in Chaco Canyon, it was rarely inhabited, its rooms used for food storage and as a place for sacred ceremony. No more than 0.2 miles past Casa Chiquita, at another hairpin turn, there are petroglyphs behind a large boulder. The spirals were made somewhere around 1,000 years ago. The animal figure was more than likely made a few hundred years ago. Some of the other markings etched on the wall are from visitors of the very recent past who could not help themselves.

The marked Petroglyph Trail, which parallels the main trail, is reached at 1.5 miles.

Peñasco Blanco

There are six different panels along this 0.3-mile stretch. The most elaborate is Panel 6, with its collection of beings, bighorn sheep, and spirals. But the most significant is Panel 4, with its supernatural figure and Katsina mask. Most of the petroglyphs are 15 to 25 feet off the ground.

Back on the main trail you hike another 0.7 mile (2.5 miles total) to reach the Chaco Wash crossing. The trail dips down into the wash and crosses it at a left bend, shortly before the main channel bends back to the right. A cluster of trees is situated next to the crossing. If heavy rains have occurred recently, the wash may be too dangerous to cross. Make sure to check with the visitor center for the most up-to-date information. Across the main channel, the trail wanders a short distance through the wash before beginning the climb to Peñasco Blanco. At 2.9 miles the trail splits. The right fork accesses the Super Nova in approximately 0.7 mile. This brilliant work of art is set in a shaded overhang of the cliff wall. The belief is that this pictograph (rock painting) may be an astronomical record from A.D. 1054 of an exploding star that we know today as the Crab Nebula.

Continuing straight, the trail winds its way up to Peñasco Blanco at 3.6 miles. In the distance to the west-northwest, you can see the natural sand-dune dam of the two washes. Stepping more to the south, once on the grounds of the ruin, you can see down the Escavado Wash to Mount Taylor. There is also a great view down Chaco Canyon. The blocky structure silhouetted above Pueblo Bonito on the mesa top to the east is New Alto.

No Relation to Elmo

Five distinct styles of masonry were used in Chaco Canyon. The oldest, as seen in much of Pueblo Bonito, consisted of a single layer of stones and a generous amount of mud mortar. When the Chacoans started building multistory structures, they employed thicker interior walls with a thin veneer. These walls tapered as they went higher to distribute the weight. The last buildings constructed in Chaco in the time period of New Alto used what is known as the McElmo style—a masonry technique in which a thinner interior wall was combined with the thicker veneer of shaped sandstone. Upon entering Peñasco Blanco, you can see three styles in one stretch of wall across to the right of the open area.

50

Pueblo Alto Loop

Type: Day hike

Season: April to November

Total distance: 5.1 miles

Rating: Moderate

Elevation gain: 350 feet

Location: Chaco Canyon National Historic Park, 48 miles south-southeast of Farmington

Maps: USGS Pueblo Bonito

Getting There

From Farmington, travel 12 miles east on US 64 to the town of Bloomfield. Turn right at the junction with US 550, heading south. At 39.2 miles down US 550, you reach the signed right turn for CR 7900. Plenty of signs along the way indicate the upcoming turn and deter you from taking other roads. In 5 miles (56.2 miles total), turn right onto CR 7950. Three miles down the surface changes from pavement to packed dirt. This road can be difficult to navigate after periods of heavy rain. At 77.1 miles, the road transitions back to pavement as you enter the park boundary. You pass by the campground to reach the visitor center at 79.7 miles. The fee is $8 per vehicle, good for 7 days. The backcountry trail book available at the visitor center is a handy companion on the hike. Following the 8-mile loop road, you pass by Pueblo Bonito to reach the short spur road and the parking area, which is directly across from Pueblo Arroyo (83.7 miles).

The Trail

No less than six of Chaco Canyon's 14 pueblos are clustered around this walk through history. Chetro Ketl and Pueblo Bonito, the two largest and most impressive ancient structures in the United States, are situated a short way after the start of this journey. Pueblo del Arroyo and Kin Kletso are within 0.2 mile of one another, followed by New Alto and Pueblo Alto. This Anazazi (ancient Puebloan people) home tour also provides overlook vistas of the surrounding landscape, including a stretch of the nearly 400 miles of roadway the Chaco people built over 1,000 years ago.

A dirt road leads beyond the wilderness check-in box to Kin Kletso in slightly more

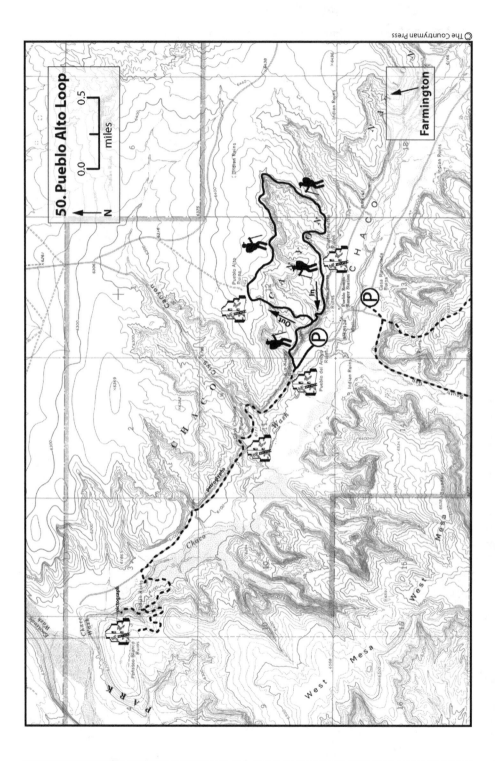

50 Hikes in Northern New Mexico

than 0.2 mile. This pueblo was constructed in the early 11th century and reflects the later McElmo building style used on other pueblos like New Alto and Pueblo Alto, situated on the mesa top beyond. The trail leads behind Kin Kletso and begins what at first appears to be an impossible course up the sheer sandstone cliff wall. With some high stepping, the trail follows a natural staircase set in a long crack in the cliff, ending atop the mesa. This is somewhat physically demanding and may not be suitable for everyone.

Now perched on the canyon rim, you have a high view across and up and down Chaco Canyon. The trail hugs the rim for the next 0.75 mile to the junction for Pueblo Alto. As mentioned earlier, the backcountry trail book available at the visitor center is worth picking up. It points out features like small carved basins used for making offerings and the fossilized shrimp and clam shells noticeable in many places across this ancient solidified sea bed. The path along the entire loop hike is marked with cairns when need be, so it's easy to follow.

At the junction, you can either continue down to the next lower level of the canyon rim to overlooks of Pueblo Bonito and Chetro Ketl or save the bird's eye overview of the grandest Great Houses for the end on the loop back. The trail moves up off the rim and onto a more vegetated mesa top. This area is a full-on desert, receiving less than 10 inches of precipitation annually, but still home to yucca, sagebrush, grease bush, prickly pear, and desert wildflowers. The simple theory for why the most majestic civilization of its time was constructed in Chaco Canyon is that the climate was different, presumably with a higher amount of moisture. There may have been years of bountiful precipitation

here, but there were also years of excessive drought, which led to one of only a few theories to explain why Chaco was left to the spirits after less than 300 years.

Climbing the Chacoan Stairs, you reach New Alto and Pueblo Alto at 1.6 miles. New Alto is off to the left. Built in A.D. 1100, its 58 rooms contained within two stories served as a seasonal residence. Straight ahead is the continuation of what is referred to as the North Road. The 30-foot-wide road leads 40 miles from here to the Salmon Ruins in present-day Bloomfield. As mentioned, the Chacoans built nearly 400 miles of roadways—this in a culture that had no domesticated beasts of burden to pull a wagon. Archeologists speculate that the roads were built for ceremonial purposes.

Pueblo Alto, next to New Alto, was only one story high and contained 70 rooms. The midden, or trash pile, roped off to the east of the ruin has been tremendously useful in determining both habits and the area's degree of use. The trail strikes out to the east, moving down canyon. Fajada Butte is visible in the distance. Toward the top of the butte is a sun calendar constructed from three large flat sandstone slabs, and a spiral petroglyph is etched in the wall behind the vertically situated stones. The spiral is struck with a shaft, or dagger, of sunlight that on the summer solstice splits the spiral down the middle. The calendar's location high on a butte over 0.5 mile from any pueblo has led archeologists to theorize that its use was more ceremonial than practical.

There are some fantastic vistas of prominent geographic features from the Pueblo Alto area, and more farther along as you move down the canyon rim. To the south, the flat-topped mesa is the now

An overview of Pueblo Bonito

dormant, but was once wildly violent Mount Taylor. The Navajo country of the Chuska Mountains lies to the west, the short La Plata Range is to the north, and the silhouetted outline of the Jemez Mountains is to the east. By 2.1 miles, the trail slips back onto the scalloped sandstone rim to make a big bend around a box canyon. In the canyon are massive sandstone boulders, cleaved from the walls by the slow action of wind and water.

Where the canyon pinches together, you are by the Jackson Staircase (2.5 miles). In the process of road construction there came points when the natural topography posed engineering challenges for the Chacoan people. The solution here was to carve out steps in the wall to reach the mesa top and areas beyond. For the modern traveler, the trail to follow passes this ancient pathway and continues along the opposite rim of the box canyon. An area called the Ramp is reached at 3 miles. A very narrow split in the mesa provides the first stage of access down to the lower rim of the canyon. The trail drops enough to give you the feeling that it will access Chetro Ketl. It doesn't actually drop that far, but it does provide a perfect overview of this 1,100-year-old pueblo ruin.

Bending around the small box canyon, the trail climbs slightly before shadowing the rim to reach the junction with Pueblo Alto at 4.1 miles. If you didn't peek over the edge and down onto the pueblo, now is your chance. To finish the hike, retrace the first 1 mile back down the natural rock staircase and by Kin Kletso to the parking area.

South Mesa Hike

Across the Chaco Wash from Pueblo Bonito is the ruin known as Casa Rinconada, which has a Great Kiva with a diameter of more than 63 feet. From here a 3.6-mile loop runs to another ruin in Tsin Kletzin. There are overviews of Chaco Canyon and views of New Alto to the north and one of the southern Chacoan roads.

Resources

Santa Fe Area

BLM–Albuquerque/Rio Puerco Field Office
435 Montano Road Northeast
Albuquerque, NM 87107
505-761-8700; www.nm.blm.gov
Cabezon Peak; Ojito Wilderness; Tent Rocks

Santa Fe National Forest Supervisor's Office
1470 Rodeo Road
Santa Fe, NM 87505
505-438-7840; www.fs.fed.us/r3/sfe
Santa Fe Baldy Loop; Nambe Lake; Atalaya Mountain; Apache Canyon to Glorieta Baldy

Pecos RS
P.O. Drawer 429
Pecos, NM 87552
505-757-6121
Truchas Peak (east); Pecos Baldy Lake Loop; Glorieta Canyon; Hamilton Mesa; Mora Flats to Hamilton Mesa Loop

Pecos NHP
P.O. Box 418
Pecos, NM 87552
505-757-6414; www.nps.gov/peco
Pecos Ruins

Las Vegas RS
1926 North 7th Street
Las Vegas, NM 87701
505-425-3534
Hermit Peak

Los Alamos Area

Cuba RD
P.O. Box 130
Cuba, NM 87013
505-289-3264
San Pedro Parks Loop

Coyote RD
HC 78 Box 1
Coyote, NM 87012
505-638-5526
Chama River Wilderness; Box Canyon; Kitchen Mesa; Cerro Pedernal; Lower Cañofes Creek

Jemez RD
P.O. Box 150
Jemez Springs, NM 87025
505-829-3535
McCauley Warm Springs to Jemez Falls

Valle Caldera National Preserve
P.O. Box 359
Jemez Springs, NM 87025
505-661-3333; www.vallescaldera.gov
Valle Caldera

Los Alamos Office
475 20th Street
Los Alamos, NM 87544
505-667-5120
Cerro Grande; Bearhead Peak; Dome Wilderness

Bandelier NM
15 Entrance Road
Los Alamos, NM 87544
505-672-3861; www.nps.gov/band
Bandelier Canyon Loop; Ruins Loop; Frijoles Falls

Española RD
1710 N. Riverside Drive
Española, NM 87532
505-753-7331
Window Rock

Taos Area

Tres Piedras RD
P.O. Box 38
Tres Piedras, NM 87577
505-758-8678
Cruces Basin Wilderness;
San Antonio Mountain

Questa RD
P.O. Box 110
Questa, NM 87556
505-586-0520
Latir Loop; Placer Creek to Gold Hill
Loop; Powderhouse Canyon; Clayton
Camp

Carson National Forest
208 Cruz Alta Road
Taos, NM 87571
505-758-6200; www.fs.fed.us/r3/carson
Wheeler Peak; Lost Lake to Horseshoe
Lake; Williams Lake

Camino Real RD
P.O. Box 68
Peñasco, NM 87553
505-587-2255
San Leonardo Lakes; Truchas Peak
(west); Trampas Lakes and Hidden
Lake; Serpent Lake

Las Vegas RS
1926 North 7th Street
Las Vegas, NM 87701
505-425-3534
Rio de la Casa Lakes Loop

Cimarron Canyon State Park
P.O. Box 185

Eagle Nest, NM 87718
505-377-6271; www.emnrd.state.nm.us
Clear Creek Canyon

Capulin Volcano NM
P.O. Box 40
Capulin, NM 88414
505-278-2201; www.nps.gov/cavo
Capulin Volcano

Farmington Area

Aztec Ruins NM
#84 County Road
Aztec, NM 87410
505-334-6174; www.nps.gov/azru
Aztec Ruins

BLM–Farmington Field Office
1235 La Plata Highway, Suite A
Farmington, NM 87401
509-599-8900; www.nm.blm.gov
Bisti Badlands; De-na-zin Wilderness

Chaco Culture NHP
P.O. Box 220
Nageezi, NM 87037
www.nps.gov/chcu
Peñasco Blanco; Pueblo Alto Loop

Web Sites

Forest Guardians:
www.forestguardians.org

Leave No Trace: www.LNT.org

National Weather Service: www.noaa.gov

New Mexico Wilderness Alliance:
www.nmwild.org

USGS maps: www.usgs.gov

Valle Vidal: www.vallevidal.com

References

Arora, David. *All That the Rain Promises, and More...: A Hip Pocket Guide to Western Mushrooms.* Berkeley, Calif.: Ten Speed Press, 1991.

Julyan, Bob. *New Mexico's Wilderness Areas: The Complete Guide.* Englewood, Colorado: Westcliffe Publishers, 1998.

New Light on Chaco Canyon. Edited by David Grant Noble. Santa Fe, New Mexico: School of American Research Press, 1984.

Noble, Grant David. *Pueblos, Villages, Forts, and Trails: A Guide to New Mexico's Past.* Albuquerque: University of New Mexico Press, 1994.

Parent, Laurence. *Hiking New Mexico.* Guilford, Connecticut: The Globe Pequot Press, 1998.

Index

A

Abiquiu, 142
Alamo Canyon, 126, 129, 130
Alamo Wash, 215–16
Alcove House, 130, 133–34
Altitude sickness, 20
Ancestral Pueblan people, 14, 133, 188, 212, 225
Animal hazards, 21
Animas River, 211, 212
Apache Canyon to Glorieta Baldy, 61–63
Apache Creek, 63
Apache tribe, 219
Arroyo de las Lamitas, 139
Arroyo del Yeso, 100
Aspen Peak, 120
Aspen Vista, 45
Atalaya Mountain, 46–48
Athabaskan people, 219–20
Augustiani, John, 80, 82
Aztec people, 212
Aztec Ruins, 211–14

B

Backpacks, 23
Baldy Mountain, 154, 204
Bandelier, Adolph F. A., 126–28, 138
Bandelier Canyon Loop, 126–30
Bandelier National Monument, 115–17, 122–23, 124, 126–38
Baneberry, 154
Barillas Peak Lookout, 42
Bass, Rick, 80
Battleship Rock, 94–95
Bearhead Peak, 118–21
Beatty's Flats, 74, 79
Beaver Creek, 144
Bernalillito Mesa, 32
Bisti Badlands, 215–17, 218

Bisti (Lucas), 216
Bisti Wilderness, 215–17, 218
Bloomfield (town), 212, 227
Bosque, 48
Box Canyon, 99–101
Bull Creek, 154, 156
Bull-of-the-Woods Pasture, 162, 164

C

Cabezon Peak, 27–29
Cabresto Lake, 151
Camposanto, 100–101
Cañones Creek, 110–11
Capulin Canyon, 130
Capulin Volcano, 206–9
Carson National Forest, 144–50, 157–61, 190
Casa Chiquita, 223
Casa Rinconada, 229
Cattle grazing, 87
Cave Creek, 55, 58, 59
Cave Kiva, 133
Caves, 35, 58
Ceremonial Cave. *See* Long House
Cerro de los Posos, 113–14
Cerro Grande, 115–17
Cerro Pedernal, 103, 106–8
Cerro Picacho, 122, 124
Chaco Canyon, 211, 212, 223, 224
Chaco Canyon National Historic Park, 221–29
Chaco Wash, 221–23, 224
Chacoan people, 14–15, 221, 223, 224, 225, 227
Chacoan Stairs, 227
Chama River Wilderness, 90–93
Chavez Canyon, 93
Chetro Ketl, 225, 227, 228
Cholla, 103

Y